Priest

Also by Michael S. Rose
from Sophia Institute Press®:

Ugly as Sin

Michael S. Rose

Priest

Portraits of Ten Good Men
Serving the Church Today

SOPHIA INSTITUTE PRESS®
Manchester, New Hampshire

Sophia Institute Press®
Box 5284, Manchester, NH 03108
1-800-888-9344

Library of Congress Cataloging-in-Publication Data

Rose, Michael S., 1969-
    Priest : portraits of ten good men serving the church
today / Michael S. Rose.
        p. cm.
    ISBN 1-928832-71-7 (pbk. : alk. paper)
    1. Catholic Church — Clergy. 2. Priesthood. 3. Catholic
    Church — Clergy — Religious life. 4. Catholic Church
    Clergy — Biography. I. Title.
BX1912 .R66 2003
282'.092'2 — dc21   2003011924

04 05 06 07 08 10 9 8 7 6 5 4 3

Contents

Introduction

The Catholic priesthood has become one of the most misunderstood callings in modern times. What is a priest? What does a priest do? Why does the Church ordain priests to be set apart from the rest of us? Is the priesthood necessary or even desirable?

Too many Catholics today have difficulty answering these simple questions. In a time when the tabloid bonanza of sexual abuse by Catholic priests dominates the news, the priesthood has become an increasingly significant and controversial topic for people of every theological persuasion. In an age when so much discussion centers on how Catholics need to learn to live without priests, many Catholics have lost sight of why Christ instituted the sacred priesthood in the first place.

The priesthood has always had its detractors — today as much as ever. It has been reviled throughout history by anti-Church reformers such as the Calvinists in Northern Europe and the so-called Nativists in North America. Anticlerical forces such as the Spanish revolutionaries of the 1930s slaughtered priests by the dozens, publicly dismembering their charred bodies; the French revolutionaries of the eighteenth century chose to roll their ordained heads through the streets.

Amid all this hatred, it remains a profound mystery to the world that an institution such as the Catholic priesthood has endured for two millennia. In the words of François Mauriac, priests "no longer have any human advantage. Celibacy, solitude, hatred very often, derision, and, above all, the indifference of a world in which there seems to be no longer room for them — such is the portion they have chosen."

The priesthood has also had its share of defenders. Stalwart Catholics, understanding the holiness of the priesthood as instituted by Christ on Holy Thursday, have never ceased to come forward in defense of their legitimate pastors. Many well-meaning Catholics, however, especially in recent decades, have tended to sugarcoat their defenses, almost as if priests did not live in the same world as the rest of us; as if they were not subject to the same laws of nature. With the aid of denial and avoidance, or through sheer ignorance, these naive defenders have ultimately done little good for the priesthood.

It has taken a series of formidable sex scandals, unprecedented in modern times, to bring many of the well-meaning to their senses, to acknowledge the stark reality. The priesthood is more than worth defending. But it's worth defending for what it is and ought to be. We simply cannot dismiss all human problems in an individual by virtue of his ordination. The Church cannot afford to deny the occurrences of abuse and failure that have brought corruption into the Catholic priesthood.

Priest, as its title suggests, is a book about the priesthood — a book written neither from the perspective of an anti-Church reformer who wants fundamentally to change or eliminate the Catholic priesthood, nor from the perspective of one who seeks to sugarcoat the sacred institution by painting an image of priests who stand head and shoulders above the rest of society simply by dint of their ordination. This book is not a mere paean to the priesthood. It is a simple and forthright look at the priesthood at the beginning of the twenty-first century, through the eyes of priests who are devoted to Christ and His Church.

Although each priest featured in the chapters that follow has played his own unique role in today's Church, together they share a number of similarities. Each understands and accepts the teachings of the Catholic Church. Each understands and accepts the role of the priest in the Church and in society. Each loves his vocation as a priest and actively encourages and promotes other such vocations. Each faithfully serves the Church, doing what priests were ordained to do: offering the sacraments, preaching the gospel, teaching the Faith, and leading souls to Christ and eternal salvation. At the same time, each understands the many challenges that confront the Church today, and the many obstacles and temptations with which priests must contend. Not one expresses himself with the intent of minimizing the challenges or downplaying the many struggles. Each understands and acknowledges that this particular calling is not for the faint of heart.

In the words of one priest: "No wimps need apply."

All is not well in the priesthood today — but neither was it in apostolic times. After all, the twelve Apostles were the Church's first priests. Peter denied Christ three times; nine other apostles were cowards who dared not follow Jesus to Golgotha; and Judas, the first "bad priest," betrayed the innocent blood of his Lord. That leaves only John, "the apostle whom Jesus loved" (cf. John 20:2). Nevertheless, it is not the priesthood that is the problem — not today and not in apostolic times. The problem is more often than not a failure of young men to hear and faithfully answer their calling; a failure of seminaries and bishops to form and educate their future priests properly; a failure of the ordained to focus on the duties of their state in life; and a failure of the laity to offer the proper spiritual and moral support for their pastoral leaders.

A warning: *Priest* deals with some of the most controversial issues in the Church and in the priesthood today, not ignoring the hard realities that threaten the integrity and mission of the priesthood: the sexual abuse of children, homosexuality, the discipline of celibacy, the lack of support received from fellow priests and bishops, and the undermining of the teachings of the Church by certain priests, as well as the connection between dissent, personal failings, and sinful behavior. Nevertheless, I hope to cover these controversial aspects of the priestly ministry without scandalizing. In fact, I believe honest coverage of these issues will help promote future vocations and strengthen the priesthood by making it healthier and more effective in its mission to the Church and to the world.

Priest

Chapter 1

Healing the Sick, Raising the Dead

"I should have been ordained at seven years old," said Fr. Albert E. Lauer. In grade school he gave his life to Jesus. He loved the Mass and received Holy Communion every day. Even during his high school years at St. Gregory's in Cincinnati, Ohio, he understood that the Holy Spirit was active in his life. When he entered college seminary, however, he began to drift. "My heart began to move away from God," he explained. "I began to sin by treasuring the pleasures of the world." Fr. Lauer explained his drifting from the Faith as "losing his first love" (after Revelation 2:4: "You have abandoned the love that you had at first"). When he was a graduate seminarian, studying to be a priest at Mount St. Mary's Seminary of the West in Cincinnati, his heart continued to move further away from God. The secular humanism of that environment — an environment in which he was training to serve the Church as "another Christ" — pushed him so far away from God that he felt spiritually at the lowest point in his life on the day of his ordination to the priesthood, May 25, 1974.

For nearly twenty years, Albert Lauer had prepared to become a priest. "Over two hundred priests laid hands on me that day," he remembered, "but I did not receive God's fullest blessings on my

3

priesthood because I stifled the Holy Spirit in my life." Little did he know at the time that the Holy Spirit would later play a major role in his life as a priest.

Part of his spiritual problem stemmed from the revolutionary atmosphere of American society in the late 1960s, a difficult time for Catholics and non-Catholics alike. Confusion reigned in the Church during those years, as theologians, liturgists, and social commentators offered a variety of interpretations of the recently concluded Second Vatican Council (1962-1965).

Fr. Lauer had grown up praying the Rosary each day. Looking back on his early years, he realized that his daily family Rosary was one of the highlights of his childhood. "Even during high school and college," he said, "Mary's prayers for me through the Rosary were a source of life and light. But in graduate school, I finally got too sophisticated for the Rosary, and I put Mary into the background of my life."

His demotion of Mary abetted his spiritual deterioration. He hardly remembers praying the Rosary at all during his first year of priesthood. He was serving as an assistant pastor at St. Luke's Church and teaching at Archbishop Alter High School in Dayton at the time. "This was probably the most miserable year of my life," he lamented. "My house was no longer built on the solid Rock of Jesus, but on the sands of selfishness. I was depressed for the first time in my life. I was going through the 'living death' which those who don't personally know Jesus must endure. My life was becoming meaningless."

During that first year, he recalled, people at both the parish and the school were gracious to him. Nevertheless, when parishioners asked him to lead them in a Sunday-evening prayer group, he couldn't bring himself to give up his couch time watching NFL football, to which he said he was addicted. "I was a television and sports addict," he admitted. He was scheduling his day more around television programs than the Holy Mass. Football, base-ball, and basketball came to dominate his thoughts — pushing Jesus and Mary further away from him.

Almost a year after his ordination, a week before Pentecost, he preached on Acts 1:14: "Together they devoted themselves to constant prayer." In his homily, he challenged parishioners to ap-ply this teaching by coming to church for prayer throughout the week to prepare for the feast of Pentecost. He didn't think people would actually come. Fr. Lauer was surprised, then, when about a dozen parishioners showed up at the church that Sunday evening. He was even more surprised when they knocked on his door and said they expected him to lead them in prayer.

"I hadn't the slightest idea what to do," he admitted. Without knowing how they did it, he and his group of parishioners prayed for an hour. Within four nights, the group had grown in number, and they were praying for three hours each evening and returning for the 6:15 a.m. Mass each morning. Fr. Lauer was astounded. What was happening, he wondered? "It was a sovereign act of God," he said, "like the baptism Cornelius and his household re-ceived" (Acts 10:44-47).

The group continued to pray each night, reading the Scrip-tures, praying spontaneously, and meditating. They almost liter-ally "prayed without ceasing" (1 Thess. 5:17) until Pentecost. "We were so happy," he remembered, "we decided to pray in thanks-giving during the week following Pentecost. After that, we prayed for another day, then another." This continued for over a year, for five hundred nightly prayer meetings.

This second year of Fr. Lauer's priesthood — 1975 — was a turning point in his life. Giving credit to an "outpouring of the Holy Spirit at Pentecost," he almost immediately returned to

Mary and took up once again the practice of praying the Rosary every day. Twice a week, he and a few parishioners would also pray the Rosary in front of a local abortion clinic, a practice he would continue for the rest of his life.

During this grace-filled second year of his priesthood, Fr. Lauer was assigned to hospital ministry, in addition to his duties at the parish. At that time, he and some parishioners started a soup kitchen to minister to the poor. They started with nothing — no place, no funds, and no food, dishes, or utensils. "We found a little hall to rent, begged some food, and opened the soup kitchen at the time of the devastating winter of 1976," he explained. "This ministry was a clear witness to the Lord's miracle-power and love for the poor."

Believing strongly that the spiritual works of mercy naturally complement the corporal works of mercy, Fr. Lauer and his prayer group also ministered to the poor by visiting and praying for the sick at their homes, in hospitals, and in nursing homes. Eventually, he said, he witnessed many "inner healings," and conversions of heart. But, for Fr. Lauer, this was only the beginning of a lifelong healing ministry that would include, not only inner spiritual healings, but physical healings as well.

"Cure the sick, raise the dead, heal the leprous, expel demons." That quotation from Matthew 10:8 was one he prayed about often after he was initiated into hospital ministry. He knew that his task was not only to comfort the sick, but also to heal them through the sacrament of the Anointing of the Sick — if it were God's will. He knew this intellectually at first, but it wasn't until he experienced the first "miraculous" healing that he acquired a deep faith in the ministry of healing in the name of Jesus: a priest is "another Christ," and part of Christ's ministry was healing the sick and the lame, and even raising the dead.

Healing the Sick, Raising the Dead

One day a woman asked Fr. Lauer to pray for a friend who was in the intensive-care unit at the local hospital. No one in recorded medical history had ever recovered from the combination of diseases this woman had. The doctors had informed her husband that she was probably already technically dead, although the machines made it appear that her body was still functioning. The doctors told him they would pronounce his wife dead that afternoon.

"When I met the husband," remembered Fr. Lauer, "he was looking through the yellow pages under 'funeral directors.' I introduced myself and mentioned that I had been asked to pray for his wife." The priest administered the Anointing of the Sick and returned later that afternoon to check on the patient. She was not pronounced dead. The doctors told him they were now going to wait until morning.

The next morning, Fr. Lauer returned to the hospital, and again the woman had not been pronounced dead. In fact, she came out of her coma a couple of days later. In two weeks she was discharged from the intensive-care unit, and a month later she left the hospital for home.

"Not only was she changed from death to life," said Fr. Lauer, "but her husband moved from skepticism to faith. From looking through the yellow pages for an undertaker, he came to looking through the Bible to meet Jesus, the Resurrection and Life, the miraculous Healer of his wife." That healing even caused a stir in the medical community. Doctors from Ohio State investigated the healing as an unprecedented event. Nevertheless, they could offer no medical explanation.

That dramatic healing prepared Fr. Lauer for a sudden transfer to Cincinnati. An emergency situation in priest personnel required his experience in hospital chaplaincy. During the year that followed, in his service to three area hospitals, he witnessed healings both quiet and dramatic. "I realized that God answers every prayer with a great outpouring of His love — not always the way we expect, but always in love, and giving us what we ask for, or better."

After his "reversion" to the Church, when he accepted the guidance of the Holy Spirit in his life, Fr. Lauer not only witnessed the great works of God, but also began to be acutely aware of the spiritual warfare exacted by the work of the Devil. When he was a seminarian, he had been assigned to teach CCD at Our Lady of Presentation in a poor section of Cincinnati, adjacent to a crime-infested housing project called English Woods. While there, he was surprised to find an all-white congregation in the midst of a predominantly black neighborhood. "The poison of racial bigotry was openly and aggressively expressed in parish meetings," he said. Despite this, he felt a strong call to that parish, and when he was assigned to hospital chaplaincy in Cincinnati, he requested that he be assigned there. The archbishop agreed.

One Sunday, not long after he arrived at Presentation, he preached against racial prejudice and announced that he would personally ask anyone who persisted in bigoted words, behavior, or attitudes to leave the church. A few parishioners left after that sermon, he remembered. Apparently there were others who quickly grew to dislike the new assistant pastor, because one day Fr. Lauer received a call from the archbishop informing him that parishioners were writing letters denouncing Fr. Lauer. When the names of those who had attacked him were divulged, he didn't even recognize many of them. "This puzzled me," he said, "since I had never experienced anything like it. How could people I hardly knew hate me so much?"

Throughout his seminary training, he had been highly secularized. For all practical purposes, he had come to deny that the Devil had any significance. Suddenly he was facing a situation for which the only reasonable explanation was the Devil. "When I read Ephesians 6:12-13, the bright shining light of God's word overcame my darkness," he said. It was then that he fully realized that his battle was not against people, but against "the rulers of this world of darkness, the evil spirits in regions above."

He began to fight the Devil and not the people, he said. "I used the spiritual weapon of prayer and received the Lord's victory, when previously I didn't even know there was a war." All the insults and attacks came to a head when he and his pastor were asked to meet with the archbishop, who ultimately gave him his full support and an encouraging vote of confidence.

Ironically, Fr. Lauer said, his time at Our Lady of Presentation Church became "the highest mountain" of God's work in his life. With the help of some parishioners, he began to intercede daily for renewal of the life of the parish. Numbers were dwindling; there were few young families and virtually no black members of the congregation. The first year of this prayer and accompanying evangelization yielded the reception of twelve men and women into the Catholic Church at the parish's Easter Vigil Mass. After a second year of hard work, prayer, and evangelization, ninety-three people returned to the Church or were received into it. These new parishioners made up some thirty percent of the entire congregation. The struggle to overcome racial prejudices in the parish also bore great fruit. Within five years, the parish consisted of white and black, rich and poor, young and old, the highly educated and the illiterate.

During the time he served as assistant pastor at Presentation, Fr. Lauer continued his chaplaincy at one area hospital. This ministry required him to own a car so that he could attend to his duties in a timely fashion. After all, he was often called in the middle of the night to confer Last Rites, including the Anointing of the

Sick. Thus, when his car broke down for dead one day, he was naturally frustrated. It would be a terrible inconvenience, he thought, and he resigned to buy a used car within a week.

During that week without a car, however, Fr. Lauer's transportation needs were taken care of smoothly. Not once did he have a problem getting where he needed to go, when he needed to be there. That being so, he postponed buying another car. Another week went by, then another, then a month, two months, and still not once did he require his own car. He had taken to hitchhiking, each day, back and forth from the hospitals!

"People were shocked to pick up a hitchhiking priest dressed in black," he said. "But one man who gave me a lift later entered the seminary." Although he was constantly chided for being "careless," not one patient was ever delayed his pastoral care. "God seemed to be calling me not to own a car," he concluded. And from that time onward, although he still drove from time to time, he never again owned a car. He looked at it this way: "Blessed are the poor in spirit; the reign of God is theirs" (Matt. 5:3). Giving up owning a car was the first step in a commitment to spiritual poverty for the sake of the Kingdom of God that he would follow thereafter.

The parish existed, not so much in spiritual poverty, but in material poverty. When Fr. Lauer arrived at Presentation Church, the weekly collections were somewhere between $200 and $300. Many people were predicting the bankruptcy of the parish, but through the fruits of fervent prayer, Fr. Lauer said, never was there a bill that went unpaid. He attributed this partly to tithing — donating a tenth of one's income — which after a year or so, most of the parishioners were doing as an act of generosity and detachment from the world.

Fr. Lauer saw God's will being followed in other ways at the parish, and he saw also the hand of God working among the parishioners. One of those ways was through Bible studies. During the eleven years that he attended seminary, he had been assigned to read the Bible daily. Nevertheless, he never took much interest in it. Although he had excelled academically in all his Scripture courses, earned three degrees, could read the original Greek of the New Testament, and began his priesthood teaching the Bible several hours a day at Alter High School, the Bible remained "a closed book" to him. "I almost never read it," he admitted, "unless I had to prepare a lesson or homily."

But after he began to follow the Lord's will and the Holy Spirit's guidance in his life, he received a deep interest in the Scriptures. He began to read the Bible constantly, even reading a verse or two at stop lights (before he gave up cars). "I was devouring the Word of God," he said. "I started teaching the Bible at prayer meetings and setting up Bible studies for adults. I eventually tripled the length of my homilies. I started training Bible teachers and set up Bible study groups all over Cincinnati and northern Kentucky." The word of God so much became his "daily bread" that he founded, wrote, and edited a periodical called *One Bread, One Body* that included meditations on the daily readings for Mass. He followed that project by producing a daily fifteen-minute radio program called *Daily Bread* that provided reflections on the Scriptures.

At the same time, Fr. Lauer made a point of encouraging his parishioners to attend Mass daily, not just on Sundays to meet their weekly obligation. As the months wore on, daily Mass attendance increased significantly. "We added an evening Mass, Monday through Friday," he explained, "to maximize the opportunity for daily Mass." He also added times each day after Mass for Adoration of the Blessed Sacrament. They began with a few hours of exposition each day, but eventually extended the adoration hours to more than forty each week.

Priest

Along with an increase in daily Mass attendance came an increase in the number of penitents confessing their sins each week. When Fr. Lauer first arrived at Presentation, hardly anyone bothered to go to Confession. He made himself available for the sacrament for an hour each week, but during most of that time he sat idle. After praying daily for a year for people to return to the practice of Confession, Fr. Lauer noticed a major change. At first, one or two people came in for Confession during that scheduled hour. Gradually more and more people started coming. In two years, the time for confessions had to be extended, and people also began to make appointments. The time Fr. Lauer spent listening to confessions increased from a few minutes each week to nearly ten hours each week.

During this time, Fr. Lauer was learning more and more about spiritual poverty, but it wasn't until his stereo was stolen that he finally embraced the principle fully. It was around Thanksgiving one year, he remembered, when, during a Mass for one of the prayer groups in the city, he had preached on the importance of simplifying one's life and appreciating the bounty of material possessions the Lord provides. When he returned to his rectory that evening, he was surprised to find a light on. When he opened the door, he saw that the office and rectory had been ransacked. In fact, he had actually walked in on the burglar, who escaped out the back door.

The thief hadn't had time to rob the office, but he did get away with a thousand dollars' worth of Fr. Lauer's stereo equipment and his violin. He had a great love for music — pop music, mainly. Before his ordination, he had even worked as a disc jockey, spinning records when he wasn't watching television. He had also learned to play the guitar and was now teaching himself to play the violin.

At first he blamed the Devil and the burglar for the robbery. As time went on, however, it seemed to him that the Lord was turning this burglary to the good by setting him free of the material possessions that had dominated his life. Never again did Fr. Lauer own a stereo. With television, stereos, and cars out of his life, he found himself able to devote himself more fully to God and to the service of his people. He discovered the great beauty of giving up the things of the world.

Observing the discipline of celibacy was another way the Lord let Fr. Lauer concentrate fully on his ministry. He had always understood celibacy in the priesthood as a practical need — God's way of freeing people for the purposes of evangelism. But he later came to a deeper understanding of celibacy as a *gift* from God. "It puts God's soldiers on the front lines in spiritual warfare," he said.

Fr. Lauer experienced that spiritual warfare not only in the Church, but also in the world, especially the crime-ridden world of his inner-city neighborhood. English Woods then had one of the worst crime rates in Cincinnati. It was a dangerous place, especially after dark. Nevertheless, Fr. Lauer treaded fearlessly throughout the neighborhood, evangelizing. He took seriously his calling to preach and teach the gospel to all in his parish boundaries. He and an evangelization team of laypersons he had formed regularly walked the neighborhood. They knocked on hundreds of doors each week — giving pause even to the Jehovah's Witnesses, who were surprised that Catholics had adopted their techniques!

One day he decided to form a procession through the streets, praying the Rosary and sprinkling everyone with holy water. Since most of the Christian neighbors were black Baptists, he worried that the Catholic procession might not be understood. But, entrusting the march to God, he went ahead with it and found some surprising results: several people turned to Jesus and later joined the Church. The march became a weekly event, which touched the lives of hundreds.

On several occasions Fr. Lauer and his evangelization team banded together to proclaim Jesus in front of a neighborhood grocery store frequented by alcoholics, drug addicts, and deranged people of every stripe. "Our men began by forming a circle on the sidewalk and prayed publicly as people rushed in and out of the store. As we shared God's word on the street, the Lord set captives free and confirmed the message with cures, signs, and wonders" (cf. Mark 16:20).

One of the most dramatic conversions Fr. Lauer experienced was that of a hardened criminal from the neighborhood. One night, Fr. Lauer came upon the man who was about to rape a woman. "I just stood there and waited for him to notice me," he remembered. When the rapist saw Fr. Lauer standing there calmly, dressed in his black clerics, wearing his Roman collar, he turned from the woman and began to yell and threaten the priest. Although the man had a gun and was waving it at Fr. Lauer, the priest stood his ground, simply repeating the name of Jesus under his breath. "I was hoping he would just go away," said Fr. Lauer, "but he shocked me by saying that he wanted to go to church."

The two walked back to the church together, and Fr. Lauer remembered that he didn't have the presence of mind to know what to do. Finally, he asked the man if he wanted to know Jesus. "No," came the reply. Then he asked if he would pray. "No," again. Next, Fr. Lauer asked him to repeat a prayer after him, but again he refused. The priest then made the Sign of the Cross and asked the man if he would make that motion. He said no once again. But when Fr. Lauer asked him if he would make the Sign of the Cross by himself where no one could see him, he said yes. The man crossed himself with his left hand and hurried out of the church.

Two weeks later, he met the man again on the street. "He ran toward me," said Fr. Lauer, "and told me Jesus had come to him and freed him. He had three vices, he explained. He was a professional thief, bound by sexual lust, and preoccupied with guns. He said Jesus freed him of two of the three vices. Later, he said he was freed from the third."

In addition to evangelization, healing ministry continued to be a priority for Fr. Lauer. He and the evangelization team would often spontaneously gather around those who were hurting and pray for them, no matter where they might be — at a parish meeting, the bus stop, the grocery store, or on the street.

Part of Fr. Lauer's healing ministry involved the "healing" of unborn babies in their mothers' wombs. He continued to pray publicly in front of abortion clinics and saw babies' lives being saved before his very eyes. Beginning in the 1980s, Fr. Lauer became a conscientious objector to the payment of federal income tax, in part because it helped fund Planned Parenthood, the perpetrator of millions of abortions. "Many Christians pray for peace and life," he said, "and pay for war and death."

Fr. Lauer's conscientious-objector status wasn't easily explainable to most people. Some thought him unpatriotic; others thought he was simply interested in keeping the money for himself. The government, obviously, was also not too understanding of his reasons for not forking over his share. At one point, he was even threatened with arrest. The archbishop called him in and instructed him to pay his taxes. But Fr. Lauer proposed another idea: if he didn't receive a salary, he wouldn't be liable for not paying taxes. Thus, a deal was struck. Fr. Lauer would continue to serve as a priest without receiving a penny in compensation. From that point on, he relied solely on the donation of necessary goods to subsist. Although it was a hardship in some ways, Fr. Lauer regarded it as just another way for him to be free to serve God as a priest in His Church.

Priest

After five years with Fr. Lauer, Presentation Church was beginning to thrive: growing in numbers, free from debt, paying all its bills, and expanding in its various apostolates. Then, inexplicably, Fr. Lauer was transferred to another assignment, the parish was closed, and the archdiocese sold the church building to a Baptist congregation.

The parish was no more, but the lives of many had been changed through the evangelical efforts of the hitchhiking priest.

The next phase of Fr. Lauer's ministry was preaching missions and retreats all over the country. He continued to receive no salary and lived above the Mary Magdalene House, a place for street people to take showers, shave, and use the restroom. He purposefully lived in this no-frills environment in another crime-ridden urban neighborhood in central Cincinnati. For the next fifteen years, he led Presentation Ministries, a special apostolate devoted to getting laypeople to answer the call to holiness in their lives. He continued his radio ministry and his publication *One Bread, One Body*. At the same time, he served as a chaplain to a homeschool community, published a Catholic newspaper, helped start a Catholic radio station, and organized a week-long Bible conference each summer. He was a full-time evangelist.

During these years, he was a frequent flyer, making evangelical trips to give evenings of reflection, missions, and retreats. But not once did he carry any money with him — aside from a quarter to make one phone call, if necessary. His motto was "Trust in the Lord; He shall provide."

In 1998, the archbishop appointed Fr. Lauer pastor of Old St. Mary's Church, the oldest parish in Cincinnati. He hadn't "applied" for the position, as is the customary procedure. In fact, no priest in the Archdiocese of Cincinnati had applied for it. Located in the crime-ridden "ghetto" of Over-the-Rhine, the parish was saddled with a whopping debt of more than $700,000. Such a precarious financial position would seem daunting to most, but for Fr. Lauer it was just another challenge to be overcome by the power of prayer and fidelity to Christ and His Church.

The initial plan was to bring the parish into the black by the end of the Jubilee Year 2000. "It would have been wonderfully symbolic of the Great Jubilee as a time of unprecedented grace," he said. Much to everyone's surprise, however, Old St. Mary's retired the parish debt almost two years *before* the goal, on Easter Sunday 1999.

Debt relief came by way of three "miracles," each attributed to prayer and fasting at the encouragement of Fr. Lauer. The first miracle came from an anonymous patron who offered $300,000 in matching funds. The second came when $128,000 in donations was raised in the extraordinarily short time of forty days.

Fr. Lauer then dedicated the first month of 1999 as the "month of God the Father." Parishioners studied the Holy Father's apostolic letter *Tertio Millennio Adveniente*, and Fr. Lauer devoted each of his January homilies to elaborating on the special role of the First Person of the Blessed Trinity. To conclude the month of God the Father, the parish prayed a novena that ended on the Feast of the Presentation of Our Lord, February 2, 1999. The following day, the parish received word of another patron who had donated $215,000 — miracle number three.

By Palm Sunday, the parish's debt had been reduced to approximately $20,000, and the remainder of the debt was retired on Easter Sunday. All this was accomplished without a capital fund drive; there were no fundraisers, pledge envelopes, bingo nights, car washes, or raffles. The parish accomplished this feat through almsgiving, prayer, and fasting — the three staples of a penitential Lent.

Fundraising was not to be the issue at Fr. Lauer's new parish. The issue, rather, was "faith-raising." This faith-raising was rooted in the traditions of the Church and was expressed through the parish's renewed efforts to evangelize, catechize, and grow in personal holiness in unity with the Universal Church.

Once Old St. Mary's was out of debt, parish resources could be spent more fully on spreading the gospel and advancing the mission of the Church in the world. Yet even before the debt was retired, Fr. Lauer had embarked on several new evangelistic outreaches: parish visitations, the catechumenate, and reviving the parish's Legion of Mary. Every Wednesday afternoon, an evangelization team shared the Faith of Jesus' Church throughout the neighborhood, which many consider to be a ghetto. He also taught catechism classes every Thursday evening. "The presentation of the Gospel message is not an optional contribution for the Church," explained Fr. Lauer. "It's the duty incumbent on her by the command of Jesus, so that people can believe. It is the truth."

Fr. Lauer also brought his pro-life zeal with him to Old St. Mary's, which is located less than two miles from the largest abortion clinic in greater Cincinnati. Every Monday and Friday morning (and sometimes on other days as well) he could be seen praying the Rosary with parishioners in front of Planned Parenthood. "Our parish is blessed to have some of the most committed and experienced pro-life leaders in the area," he said, "so it wasn't difficult to initiate the pro-life activities here that should be a part of every parish."

Perhaps his two most palpable contributions to Old St. Mary's were the re-opening of the parish school and the founding of a parish-run crisis pregnancy center. Because Catholics had moved out of the city and into the suburbs many decades ago, Old St. Mary's School, which opened in 1841, closed its doors in the late 1950s.

Healing the Sick, Raising the Dead

But in 2001, Fr. Lauer re-opened the building as St. Peter Claver Latin School for Boys. "Teenage boys dominate the ghetto," he said, "and if we can get them working and living for Christ, we'll change this neighborhood, which is the most drug-ridden and crime-ridden neighborhood in the city."

Because the neighborhood is home to such dynamics, Fr. Lauer understood the need to aid women during their pregnancies and after the birth of their children, not only materially, but spiritually as well. In less than two years, the Old St. Mary's pregnancy center became the largest single service for pregnant women in the city. "It is another opportunity for us to evangelize to the neighborhood," he said. "It's a way to introduce the unchurched to Jesus."

Although the neighborhood was rough and crime was always on the rise, Fr. Lauer stood fearless through his years in service at Old St. Mary's. One of his oft-cited mottoes, popularized by Pope John Paul II, was "Be not afraid" — and he certainly took that sentiment to heart.

In April 2001, Cincinnati was racked by rioters and looters who swarmed the city streets, vandalizing buildings and attacking people at random, supposedly in protest of the police department's treatment of black criminals. The hardest-hit neighborhood was the one surrounding Old St. Mary's. One day during the riots, Fr. Lauer heard the commotion of rioters running on one of their senseless rampages down Main Street, half a block from the church. The neighbors had all boarded up their storefronts and had locked themselves safely in their stores and apartments. But not Fr. Lauer.

The priest, dressed in his black clerics and Roman collar, stood outside the church on the front steps and prayed silently as the mass of rioters wreaked havoc down the street. They ran past him, not more than ten feet away. A few saw him and stopped briefly to say that they were sorry for the way they were acting. "I never thought I'd be hearing confessions out there," he said. Seeing the priest praying serenely among the mass of crazed rioters was obviously a witness to the criminals themselves. No one touched Old St. Mary's, not that day or any other. The church and its rectory and school remained unharmed. Fr. Lauer, too, was untouched and unharmed. He had put his motto to the test.

Sadly, the week of rioting coincided with Holy Week that year. The police imposed a public curfew, prohibiting people from leaving their homes after 8 p.m. Consequently, the archbishop canceled all Easter Vigil services, which typically begin after sunset. He did not want Catholics to be arrested on the way home from Mass.

Fr. Lauer had another solution. He invited parishioners to arrive at the church before the 8:00 curfew in order to keep the Easter Vigil Mass, one of the most important services of the year. Those who attended, however, would have to remain at the church until 5:30 the next morning to avoid breaking curfew. Thus, Old St. Mary's was the only parish in the city that held the Easter Vigil Mass that year, with Fr. Lauer offering the Sacrifice of the Mass to the sound of helicopters swooping low over the church.

Not long after that Easter, Fr. Lauer discovered he had a life-threatening case of liver cancer. Many prayed for the healer to be healed, but through it all, Fr. Lauer resigned himself to do God's will. If it were God's will for him to die, he would accept that and try to be as purified a soul as possible to meet his Maker. It turned out that God's will was that Fr. Lauer leave his earthly ministry. In his final months, he continued to live in his room at the rectory. When he finally became unable to walk down the stairs and into the church to celebrate daily Mass, he celebrated Mass in his room from his bed, invited parishioners to attend, and even delivered a homily each day in his hushed, weakened voice.

During the writing of this book, Fr. Lauer died peacefully in his bed at Old St. Mary's, living out to the end his favorite motto: "Be not afraid!"

Chapter 2

The Conversion Specialist

"Perhaps the Princeton community and society at large should advise McCloskey to take to drinking nothing but the semen of AIDS patients," wrote one undergraduate student from Princeton University in the pages of the official campus newspaper. The subject was Fr. C. John McCloskey III, serving at the time as assistant chaplain at the elite Ivy League university in New Jersey. The controversy: the priest had written a letter to the *Daily Princetonian* objecting to a skit performed on campus by "performance sexeducator" Suzi Landolphi, author of *Hot, Sexy, and Safer*. The comedienne's routine was designed to promote "safer sex" and included having female students stretch oversized condoms over the heads of male classmates while an amused audience cheered them on.

Fr. McCloskey had objected to, among other things, Landolphi's view that students were "salivating animals" who lacked any sense of self-control. For this, the Princeton chaplain was publicly castigated for wanting to "enslave" women in "the holy bond of Matrimony" and for "keeping them barefoot, pregnant, and in the kitchen." This incident was just one among many incited by Princeton students and faculty who objected to

Fr. McCloskey's presence on the campus of the nation's fourth-oldest college.

Such intemperate criticism, some of which can get very nasty, is all in a day's work for a campus chaplain at a prestigious school such as Princeton, Fr. McCloskey explains in a sanguine tone. "Almost unquestioningly in the elite universities, the environment is generally not hospitable to Catholicism." The values propounded by such schools are in fact "radically anti-Christian." He had his work cut out for him from day one.

Although Fr. McCloskey himself attended an Ivy — Columbia University in New York City — he unabashedly claims that such schools "are where the seeds of the culture of death are planted." That's why he considers his ministry as chaplain on the campuses of Yale and Princeton as missionary work at the heart of the culture of death.

In 1985, Fr. McCloskey began commuting to Princeton's campus three days a week from his home in New York's Upper West Side. Not long afterward, he was appointed assistant campus chaplain at the Aquinas Institute, Princeton's equivalent to a Newman Center — educating and ministering to Catholic students. He replaced a controversial Jesuit priest who had attracted an unlikely following among Princeton students; in a relatively short period, however, Fr. McCloskey became arguably more controversial — not for departing from Catholic teaching, as his predecessor had apparently done, but for upholding it.

Partly because of his association with Opus Dei — an organization often accused of being "secretive" and "controversial" — and partly because he refused to water down Catholicism on campus, Fr. McCloskey attracted some vocal critics who claimed his approach to religion was offensive and oppressive, and that he was trying to establish a "universal hegemonic view" because he dared to disagree with the politically correct views propounded in the academic Ivory Tower. In particular, his insistence on maintaining traditional Catholic teaching on human sexuality incurred strident opposition by an on-campus faction, including well-known faculty members who went so far as to call for his removal from campus ministry.

What bothered his detractors most was that many Catholics on campus found his authentic Catholic message attractive and that he was making converts and drawing Catholic students closer to Christ and His Church. For this, Fr. McCloskey was seen as dangerous and harmful to the status quo. "In a place like Princeton, when you make waves," he says, "get ready. There's going to be opposition." Fr. McCloskey knew as much going into the job. In addition to his four years as an undergraduate at Columbia, he had also worked in the cutthroat environment of Wall Street, so he had no illusions about the challenges he would face at Princeton.

The anti-McCloskey faction there claimed that he was overly negative, rigid, and censorious. Translation: they were offended that he was placing an emphasis on personal sin, and counseling students to avoid the near occasions of sin, which are common on just about any college campus. Despite the school's reputation for "diversity" and "openness," it's ironic that some members of the Princeton community wanted Church and university authorities to suppress Fr. McCloskey because they found his views on religion and morality distasteful. They accused him of wanting to stamp out those who disagreed with him, yet they tried to silence him by demanding his expulsion. And in the end, they got their wish: in 1990 the head chaplain, a Catholic priest from the Trenton Diocese, decided to dismiss Fr. McCloskey for being too controversial.

Although no longer an official university chaplain, Fr. McCloskey moved to Princeton to serve as chaplain of the Opus Dei–owned Mercer House, just three blocks from the campus ministry office. In that capacity he continued to assist students and others, just as he had done as an official chaplain.

"A little orthodoxy seems to scare a lot of people," he commented when asked why some folks in Princeton, New Jersey, including Catholic priests, were paralyzed by anxiety at his presence. Campus ministry is about catechetics and evangelization, he says, and orthodoxy — belief in and adherence to the teachings of the Catholic Church — is the main ingredient. Using this logic, it stands to reason that without orthodoxy, campus ministry is rendered ineffectual. And that's just how he characterizes the chaplaincies at most American colleges and universities in the last several decades.

"The general situation of most campus ministries is troubled," he says. "They often find themselves understaffed through the ever-decreasing availability of qualified priests and religious. In more than a few cases, campus chaplaincies have been used as either dumping grounds or refuges for priests or women religious who have not fit in well with their dioceses or communities." From Fr. McCloskey's vantage point, "rare is the college chaplaincy that has a coherent plan for total evangelical and catechetical work with all the Catholic students from a lively, orthodox viewpoint."

That's exactly what Fr. McCloskey tried to bring to his own approach to campus ministry: a coherent plan for evangelization and catechesis from a lively, orthodox perspective. He was working, he says, in the "most exotic pagan mission territory in the world," and his goal was to "re-evangelize" a society wherein the past several generations of Catholics were not properly educated in the Faith. For this reason he believes that, after seminary, the college chaplaincy is the single most important ministry in any diocese. These "elite universities" are the places from which the future leaders of the nation will naturally emerge, Fr. McCloskey says. "These people are the best educated and the most ready to take up leadership positions, which is how we transform the culture."

Again, these schools present certain challenges that we may not find in the typical American parish. Fr. McCloskey likens the situation on today's campuses such as Princeton and Yale to a sort of "raw paganism," wherein conversions and reconciliation are always ripening for the harvest. That virtue of hope is what spares Fr. McCloskey the discouragement that many Christians feel in such places that have been routed by the forces of secularism, consumerism, and hedonism.

Simply put, he believes that it's necessary to teach college students what the Church teaches and that evangelizing means introducing them to Jesus Christ. Given the ignorance of the Catholic Faith displayed by many, if not most, college students — even on the elite campuses where students are presumably well-educated and generally intelligent — this is an obvious starting point. "It's a lot of fun, and challenging," Fr. McCloskey says, "because the students are at a point in life when they are looking for answers." Many are jaded and tend toward sophomoric cynicism, some are materialistic, but there are others who are looking for some ideals, searching for truth. The opportunity to expose them to Christian orthodoxy and the Catholic Church, Fr. McCloskey adds, is an "absolute joy."

In his experience at Princeton and Yale, many of the students came from small families who did not help them grow in the virtues of service, responsibility, and sharing that often come from growing up in a large family. These families are marked by "contraceptive selfishness" and place an emphasis on material gratification and professional success, he says. "Hedonism, prestige, security, power, and ambition are the standards by which they live." To be sure, there is no shortage of ideologies on campuses across the country that cater to such anti-Christian vices. For that reason, Fr. McCloskey also views his evangelical and catechetical mission as countercultural. Put simply, he says, a spiritual war is being waged between good and evil. The "civilization of love" that Pope John Paul II has been encouraging for two decades must combat the dominant "culture of death." The college chaplaincy, says Fr. McCloskey, is one important front on that battlefield.

He believes the first battle to be waged is against ignorance. Many students he has met with over the years seem to think that, just because they attended twelve years of Catholic schools or CCD programs, they have an adequate grasp of Church doctrine and morals. More often he found that the opposite was the case. The students knew little about the Catholic Faith, and what little they did know was often distorted by confused notions.

Consequently, the Catholic students were often the most difficult to educate. They've been misled and misinformed by poor Catholic catechetical programs in their parishes and schools. They've received little substantive instruction from the pulpit or in their religion classes.

The situation would not be quite so tragic, Fr. McCloskey says, "if it were not for the fact that often those who have been deformed come prepared to insist on their own vision of Christianity rather than to learn and adhere to the teachings of Christ and His Church." Conversely, public- and private-school students, he has found, are often much more open to the true teachings of Catholicism. Either way, most students, he says, have a desperate need of intellectual and moral answers to the challenges and pressures around them.

The Conversion Specialist

The second battle to be fought in the campus chaplaincy is an uphill one. So much of what occurs in the life of a college student, Fr. McCloskey explains, subjects him to intense pressure to conform with the world, to follow the anti-Christian principles that seem to dominate our culture — principles that place a premium on personal autonomy and self-fulfillment and often involve the abuse of sexuality.

Academic pressure confronts the student in another way. Most of the courses he will take during his time on campus will not be taught from a Christian standpoint, and many may even mock or ridicule basic Christian values. Likewise, the professors charged with guiding the student's academic progress and grading his work are often generally hostile toward Christian doctrine and morals. The books the student will read typically share the professors' viewpoints and will sometimes subtly — or even overtly — undermine the Catholic Faith.

"If the college students of today are 'baptized pagans,' " says Fr. McCloskey, it is for the chaplaincy staff to catechize them and help them live their Christian lives fully at college in the midst of their studies and personal relations, preparing them to take on even greater responsibilities in the future with their families and professional work."

Thus, the main end of the chaplaincy, he continues, is to help each student to be reconciled with God and the Church, and to help him to remain and grow in the state of grace. "A student who makes a regular practice of Communion and Confession in college will tend to carry these practices into later life and communicate them to his family and friends." The means to this main end are simple: evangelization, catechesis, and the sacraments.

As a Catholic chaplain, Fr. McCloskey received a list of the Catholic students registered at the school that year. His first step was to make contact with each of them by either calling or writing to them. In this, he followed the example of Msgr. William Nolan, the late long-time chaplain at Dartmouth College, who, during his tenure there, brought many undergraduates to the Faith through conversion. With this initial contact, he generally encouraged the student to meet with him for fifteen minutes. "In my experience," says Fr. McCloskey, "it was quite rare for the student to turn down this gesture of interest and friendliness on the part of the chaplain." These initial meetings, he says, were crucial to opening up communication with the students early in the school year. If a student is going to withstand the societal and peer pressures of campus life, he needs the countervailing help of other convinced Catholics, both clerical and lay, right from the beginning of his college career. This was a time-consuming and arduous task for Fr. McCloskey, he admits, but one that paid immediate dividends for individual students and for the vitality of the campus apostolate.

In these initial meetings, or interviews, he asked each student about his religious life and practice, to get a good sense of what was required to help him live out his life as a Christian. For many of these students, he says, the largest obstacle was that they hadn't validly received the sacrament of Penance in some years. Consequently, one of Fr. McCloskey's first tasks was to re-educate each student about the sacrament and how to conduct an examination of conscience. This was typically the first step to getting the student re-involved with the sacraments on a regular basis. To this end, he emphasizes the importance of keeping regular hours in the confessional and not simply by appointment.

Offering such advice does not come without criticism — at least it didn't at Princeton. Fr. McCloskey was accused (by other priests!) of "coercing" students into going to Confession, and using interviews with freshman students to "manipulate" them. But these priests, according to Fr. McCloskey, were simply upset that he emphasized the sacrament of Reconciliation, even though it's the duty of priests at times, he explains, to tell certain people that they're in need of Confession. In fact, he sees this as a spiritual work of mercy.

The ultimate goal of the interview, he explains, was to elicit a commitment from the student to learn more about his Faith. He encouraged this by handing out copies of the *Catechism* and the New Testament, while pointing out to each student that his knowledge of the Faith should at least be on the same level as his secular studies.

Following this initial interview, some students became involved in some of the activities of the campus chaplaincy, including Sunday Mass and sometimes daily Mass. Fr. McCloskey offered courses in Catholicism and periodic retreats with plenty of room for spiritual direction. But the two practices he promoted above all — and still does — are the daily habits of mental prayer and spiritual reading. His hope was that he could gradually help the student to a fuller life of piety: daily Mass, devotion to the Blessed Virgin, examination of conscience, and yes, the habit of making a regular confession.

At Princeton, Fr. McCloskey always kept a list of recommended reading material, not only of spiritual and literary classics written by great lights such as Newman, Chesterton, and Dante, but also informative books written from a Christian perspective that shed light on contemporary issues.

He also made lists of recommended courses at Princeton each year. Although that may sound innocuous, the anti-McCloskey faction twisted his intentions by claiming that the priest was warning students against taking particular courses. The only evidence they produced to substantiate this claim was a memo from

Fr. McCloskey that accompanied the list. The memo stated, "Remember, everything depends on the outlook of the teacher giving the course. The latter may seem quite interesting and stimulating, but if it is given by an anti-Christian, its impact is counterproductive." For this, Fr. McCloskey was blasted for "censorship" and was said to be violating the very nature of free inquiry. His critics claimed that he had no right to evaluate university courses, no matter how obliquely. In short, Fr. McCloskey's work was seen as detrimental to the welfare of the university.

Such incidents merely confirm the ongoing cultural battle in academia. A priest who fulfills his duties of teaching, preaching, and administering the sacraments — and doing it well — can expect the sort of attacks that Fr. McCloskey has endured throughout his tenure as a campus chaplain. But the payoff, he says, far outweighed any problems instigated by those who sought to stifle his ministry and influence. The "payoff" is not always concrete and measurable, but without fail, he says, from among those students who remain close to the chaplaincy, there have come vocations, and not only to the priesthood and religious life, but also to a fully dedicated lay life. "The role of the chaplaincy is to serve as an instrument of God to transmit that call to the student," he says. That's how Fr. McCloskey approached his task.

The Opus Dei priest remained in Princeton until 1998, when he "graduated" to his hometown of Washington, D.C., to take over the direction of the Catholic Information Center (CIC), which he calls a "downtown center of evangelization." Instead of ministering to college students, his focus now is winning the hearts of busy — and often cynical — Washingtonians, from fast-food employees to U.S. senators.

"It's a kind of surrogate parish," he says of the CIC. Giving "evenings of recollection," retreats, courses on Catholicism, and individual spiritual direction keeps him to a busy, fast-paced schedule. For the past few years, he has given spiritual direction to an average of twenty-five men and women each week, usually during half-hour meetings with him at his downtown office. "My basic attitude," he says, "is that I never turn down anyone. Everyone is worthy of my attention as a priest." Obviously he has been frequently recommended as a priest who is trustworthy, discreet, and orthodox in his views and in his practice of the Faith. When a priest does his job well, he'll be sought out.

As much as he's sought out, he's also accessible — in person, by phone, and by e-mail. In fact, he takes the time to answer hundreds of questions and queries about the Catholic Faith each month that come to him via the Internet. His website, "McCloskey's Perspectives" (www.frmccloskey.com), on which he posts every article he has written — and he has written many — keeps him visible and accessible. Part of his mission at the CIC, and anywhere he has ever been or will be, is catechesis. To this end, Fr. McCloskey is not at all afraid to make use of the newest and most powerful means of communication the world has to offer.

"I have a product to sell; I find prospects, and then I go after them," he explains by way of analogy. "My product is the Catholic Faith. I'm an open book. I have no secrets. I like to write articles that explain what I do." One article, entitled "Winning Converts," explains Fr. McCloskey's passion for converting souls, but, more important, explains why and how each and every Catholic can and should go about the work of making converts. "As followers of Christ," he writes, "we are interested not in winning arguments, but only in our personal 'gift of self,' which is never more complete than when we act as God's collaborators in communicating the gift of divine life, God's grace." Following in the footsteps of Catholic philosopher Dietrich von Hildebrand, Fr. McCloskey looks upon all the people he encounters each day as Catholics *in re* (in fact) or *in spe* (potentially).

Indeed, such an approach has made Fr. McCloskey a name as a "specialist" in the business of transforming souls. "Oftentimes," he explains, "those in Washington who are interested in the Catholic Faith don't know where their local parish church is or who their pastor is. So they come to me at a highly visible place in downtown Washington." These men and women are often Evangelicals and Jews. "They want a specialist," he says, "not a general practitioner. I'm a specialist in conversions, not by choice, but by reality."

As a specialist, he eschews the more institutional approach to conversion that has unfortunately become the order of the day. "Many people are turned off by the bureaucratic approach that says, 'Hey, if you want to be Catholic, you have to come here every Tuesday night for a year,' or even worse, 'Sorry, our convert program started in late August, so you'll have to wait for next year.' " The CIC was set up, in part, to give the kind of individual attention that Fr. McCloskey believes each personal conversion often requires. "I tailor-make my approach to each individual, considering his circumstances, and try to find out what's best for him," he says.

His record speaks for itself: Fr. McCloskey has aided in the conversions of some noteworthy personalities, including Kansas Senator Sam Brownback, Wall Street economist Lawrence Kudlow, political commentator Robert Novak, and conservative publisher Alfred S. Regnery. Throughout his life, he has been in contact with high-profile people on the East Coast. "That's been my line of fire, so to speak," he admits.

One of his most noteworthy conversions is that of former Jewish abortionist Dr. Bernard Nathanson. As chronicled in Nathanson's

1996 book *The Hand of God*, he was involved in abortion for nearly three decades, beginning in 1945, when he persuaded a pregnant girlfriend to abort their child. He became the director of New York's largest abortion clinic and a cofounder of the National Abortion Rights Action League. His venture into what he calls "the Satanic world of abortion" included aborting his own child. "What is it like to terminate the life of your own child?" he wrote in his book. "I have aborted the unborn children of my friends, my colleagues, casual acquaintances, even my teachers. There was never a shred of self-doubt, never a wavering of the supreme self-confidence that I was doing a major service to those who sought me out." By the time he was convinced to leave the abortion industry — moved by the images afforded by ultrasound technology — he had presided over seventy-five thousand abortions.

Functioning as an agnostic, he first converted to the pro-life cause. But for more than a decade, he walked on the brink of despair, contemplating whether to commit suicide. After witnessing an Operation Rescue demonstration at a Manhattan abortion clinic, he started to ask questions about God, and his reading interests eventually turned toward Catholic authors. "[Fr. McCloskey had] heard I was prowling around the edges of Catholicism," wrote Nathanson. "He contacted me, and we began to have weekly talks. He'd come to my house and give me reading materials."

One of the most important aspects about the priest's approach to Dr. Nathanson was that he spoke what the doctor calls "the language of reason and erudition." He was able to unite faith and reason for Nathanson, who said he needed the safety net of reason for his leap of faith. "He guided me down the path to where I am now," he said of Fr. McCloskey, when he was received into the Church by John Cardinal O'Connor in 1989. "I owe him more than anyone else."

Priest

Now operating just blocks away from the White House, Fr. McCloskey has been disparagingly called "the Catholic Church's K Street Lobbyist." But the priest takes no offense and accepts the cynical label. Why not? He is, after all, lobbying for souls. And not just the souls of the rich and influential, he says, because for every high-profile conversion like a Nathanson or a Novak, there are dozens of everyday people who convert to the Catholic Faith under his guidance.

Perhaps because of the prominence of his present assignment, Fr. McCloskey has also become one of the nation's leading priestly pundits and probably the lone self-described "conservative" Catholic priest among those who are regularly consulted by the national mainstream media on issues pertaining to the Catholic Church. He has appeared on an impressive number of television and radio programs, explaining Church teaching and defending the Catholic Faith. He has even locked horns on national television with the likes of Gary Wills and Fr. Richard McBrien. He's also often quoted in highly visible newspapers such as the *Wall Street Journal*, the *Washington Post*, and the *New York Times*.

One of the main messages he likes getting through in the press is that the Catholic Church will be revitalized in this country by a return to the traditional teachings of the Church. This stands in marked contrast to the relentless push for liberalization in doctrine and discipline as a means of solving problems in the Catholic Church. Such a message brings with it not a little ridicule and mockery and some particularly harsh criticism from Catholic liberals, but nothing Fr. McCloskey hasn't been able to take in stride.

Just as during his years in Princeton, he must regularly field criticisms of his methods and beliefs. Plenty of that criticism centers on his being a priest of Opus Dei. Critics of this international Catholic group (officially known as a "personal prelature")

that is officially recognized by the Pope claim that Opus Dei is secretive and cult-like in its practices. Fr. McCloskey dismisses such
criticism, explaining that most of Opus Dei's critics just don't understand that Catholics can dedicate themselves to God as laypersons. "That idea is so weird to them that they think Opus Dei is
like Jim Jones giving them poison to drink," he explains. Rather,
he describes the organization as a "supernatural family in the
Church" that promotes the universal call to holiness in all states
of life.

Fr. McCloskey joined Opus Dei when he was a sixteen-year-old
student at St. John's College High School in Washington, D.C.
Ironically, he was attracted to the secularity of the group and the
basic idea that one need not be a priest or a religious to live a holy
life. Indeed, he says, as a child, he never had role models who were
priests. In fact, a good number of the priests he knew in the 1960s
were rather poor examples of the priesthood. Some left, while others stayed in the Church and subverted Catholic doctrine.

Fr. McCloskey remained active in Opus Dei throughout his
college years at Columbia University, while working twenty-five
hours a week for Citibank on Wall Street. In school and in work,
he says, he was always conscious of overtly living out his life as a
Christian. With the help of his spiritual director, he discerned that
he was being called to the priesthood, a call that he found surprising, since he had always been impressed with Opus Dei's primary
focus of living out the Christian life as a layman.

From Manhattan he went overseas to attend seminary at the
epicenter of the Catholic Church: Rome. At the Roman College
of the Holy Cross, the formation center for Opus Dei priests, the
future Fr. McCloskey lived with 160 men from sixty countries
around the globe. "I can't think of any disadvantages of studying
in Rome," he says. "I was in the middle of European culture, near

the Roman martyrs, and near to the two-thousand-year history of Christendom." From there he went on to graduate study at the University of Navarre in Spain.

Although he appreciated his years in seminary, where he was influenced by the living example of his professors, he's quick to tell people that he got much more out of his years in Manhattan on Wall Street and at Columbia University than from his seminary experience. "That's what's made it so much easier to deal with people like Lawrence Kudlow or Bernard Nathanson, or street people from Harlem, for that matter. It's a lot different than a young man who went to Catholic high school, then Christendom College, and on to Mount St. Mary's Seminary. I'm not at all against that, but in a way, that man may be a little out of touch with some of the realities he'll have to face later in his priesthood."

Washington, D.C., and New York City have shaped the man who became Fr. C. John McCloskey III when he was ordained in Rome in 1982. "I'm not an angry man," he assures, but neither is he cowed by the media or academe. He's armed and dangerous — armed with the Catholic Faith and dangerous to the enemies of that Faith. "Priests are warriors for Jesus Christ," he says. "They are the Navy Seals, the Army Rangers, and the Green Berets of the Catholic Church, and I'm proud to serve among her ranks."

Chapter 3

Replanting the Seeds of Christianity
at the Ends of the Earth

In the early twentieth century, the Russian Far East boasted a thriving Catholic population. The land was populated, in addition to Russians, by Poles, Lithuanians, Germans, and other ethnic Catholics who had built thriving schools and hospitals, as well as beautiful churches. In 1917, all that changed. The Russian Revolution effectively dismantled the Catholic Church — and all of Christianity, for that matter — in this area, which later became part of the Soviet Union.

Under the leadership of Joseph Stalin, the Russian Far East became a showplace of the new Communist era: a land without churches in a country that had vanquished God. All Catholic churches were confiscated by the Soviet government. Those not razed by Communist dynamite were transformed for profane purposes: to be used as a horse barn, a movie theater, a nightclub, or a venereal-disease clinic, for example.

According to KGB statistics, between 1917 and 1937, an estimated two hundred thousand clergy and religious were executed for the Faith in Russia, their bodies thrown into mass graves. Further, the Catholic cemeteries dotted with their cross-tipped tombstones were destroyed, and the sacred ground over the graves was turned into amusement parks in city centers, the dead trodden upon by new Soviet-reared generations of children. This was all part of the strict Communist regimen of desecration that succeeded in tearing future generations away from that which put them in the presence of God.

In 1992, one month after the fall of the Soviet Union, Fr. Myron Effing arrived in Russia to help re-establish the Catholic Church in this spiritually impoverished land. At the behest of the Most Rev. Joseph Werth, the newly appointed Bishop Apostolic Administrator of Novosibirsk in Siberia, Fr. Effing was invited to establish a residence in Vladivostok, the Russian Far East's largest city. Among a population of nearly one million souls, he found fewer than ten baptized Catholics. Only a handful of others were scattered thinly throughout the rural areas of the region.

Fr. Effing and one other American priest were charged with the daunting task of re-establishing Catholic parishes in a territory twice the size of the continental United States. It is from this port city on the Sea of Japan, near volatile North Korea and Communist China, that the Evanston, Indiana, native has been serving Christ and His Church as a Catholic priest for the past decade.

The size of the territory, however, was not the most difficult impediment to Fr. Effing's new mission. Seventy-five years of militant atheism had taken its toll on the Russian population. When he arrived in Russia, he found that the vast majority of its citizens knew very little about God and virtually nothing about the Catholic Faith. This atheism, combined with the failed promises of Communism, had produced a country plagued by the worst societal ills imaginable.

"We've had to start from the ground up," he says. "Communism breeds jealousy and self-interest. Trying to teach people to be

Christian after so many years of repression and evil is really a daunting task."

His main duty as a missionary in Russia is to serve the needs of Catholics, particularly by administering the sacraments. But a further and even more difficult task is to proclaim the Good News of Jesus Christ to a culture in which most people have been taught that Jesus is a myth that was contrived to exploit people and keep them enslaved in poverty.

Those who are of middle age, explains Fr. Effing, have been disappointed by the promises of Communism. Consequently, they don't believe in anything, much less in God. "Of course they don't know much about religion," he says. "They accepted the ideology that religion is always old-fashioned, out for gold, and a throwback compared with modern ideas."

Women in Russia have been devastated by state-funded abortion — Russian abortion rates are six times higher than in the West — and in many places, the family as traditionally understood in Christianity has nearly ceased to exist. The problem of abandoned street children has grown to epic proportions. Divorce is rampant, and adultery is commonplace. "Children have had two or three 'fathers,' " Fr. Effing laments, "but very few brothers or sisters."

And these children have been exposed in recent decades to the worst elements of Western culture that have infiltrated the Russian Far East: pornography, rock music, and drugs. An essay by Sergey Cherednichenko of Vladivostok in the Russian newspaper *Pravda* described the situation this way:

Each of us meets them practically every day, in stores, in public transport, in elevators of our own homes. Numerous groups of teenagers with impudent glances, stupid grins on their faces, with unduly familiar manners idling about the streets of Russian cities. They always have a box of cigarettes, a bottle of beer, or a syringe in their pockets. Or probably even a knife! Did you ever see them? They are abandoned even by their own parents in the ruthless everyday survival race. . . .

Schools also pay little attention to upbringing of the youth; teachers in Russia are in a desperate situation themselves because of non-payment of wages. The Education Ministry cares mostly about raising school marks, not about the upbringing of the younger generation.[1]

All these societal ills create an immense challenge for a priest in post-Communist Russia, one that cannot be overstated. The challenge was compounded by the fact that, when Fr. Effing first arrived in Vladivostok, he spoke not a word of Russian, which he describes as "the most difficult language in the world." But that didn't deter him from what he saw as his mission to serve.

"When it became possible for priests to go again to Russia," he says, "I reasoned that many would come from Ireland and Poland, where there were vocations, but obviously they would work mostly in European Russia. So I thought that Americans should work in the Far East, especially because of the Russian connections with America in Alaska and California." At the time, a weekly direct flight from San Francisco to Khabarovsk facilitated travel between the western United States and Siberia. Since Fr. Effing was living in northern California at the time, it was clear to him that if he was going to serve in the former Soviet Union, his calling was to the Russian Far East.

---

[1] Sergey Cherednichenko, "Thoughts About Generations to Come," *Pravda*, December 17, 2002.

Replanting the Seeds of Christianity

When he first arrived, he was surprised at how little he knew of this part of the world and what life was like there, despite the fact that he had once taught world geography. His first impression of Russia was at the airport in Khabarovsk: "When I flew to Magadan from Khabarovsk, there were live chickens with us in the plane, so I felt as though I were flying in the bush in Africa."

Upon arrival in Vladivostok, he met a handful of Catholics who had written to Bishop Werth asking for a priest. They took Fr. Effing to the imposing nineteenth-century Gothic-style edifice that was built to serve as the Catholic cathedral, but had been confiscated by the Communists following the revolution nearly sixty years before. There he celebrated his first Mass in Vladivostok, on the street, at the front door, along with about fifteen others.

For the first two years in the city, Fr. Effing was forced to rent various halls to celebrate a public Mass on Sundays. In January 1994, however, ownership of the old cathedral was returned to the Catholic Church after two years of bureaucratic and political struggles. This was only the second such church in all of Russia to be given back to the Catholic Church. Thus, Fr. Effing felt this was quite an accomplishment at the time.

"Like everything else under Communism, the cathedral was allowed to decay to the point where it needed major construction before it could become a beautiful place for worship again," says Fr. Effing. For the past eight years, part of his mission to re-establish the Catholic Church has been to refurbish this church, which is the only Catholic building within a radius of one thousand miles that was built as a house of worship. Most other churches and synagogues were demolished by the Communists long ago.

During the time the cathedral was used as a government building for Communist archives, one additional wooden floor and two reinforced concrete floors were built into it. In November 1994, workmen began to remove the upper concrete floor where Fr. Effing, along with about a hundred worshipers, had celebrated Mass for the previous eleven months. Sunday Mass was eventually moved to the ground floor. Then the work of restoration began.

"Some people are opposed to spending large amounts of money on buildings," admits Fr. Effing, "but that's probably because there are already many churches in America. But the former cathedral of Vladivostok is the only active Catholic church with church architecture in a radius of more than 2,500 miles."

For Fr. Effing, restoring the cathedral and even finishing off the steeple and installing bells — the bells have already been donated by the Solidarity movement of Poland — is just the beginning. He is also working actively toward making Vladivostok a center of Catholic study, perhaps even with a seminary and a Catholic university.

By 1996, four years after founding Most Holy Mother of God parish at the Vladivostok cathedral, the number of Catholics had grown from eight to nearly three hundred, some of whom traveled as much as two hours to get to Mass on Sundays. Besides the Vladivostok parish, Fr. Effing also founded Immaculate Conception in the city of Khabarovsk, a fourteen-hour train ride from his home in Vladivostok; Sts. Cyril and Methodius in Nicholaevsk-on-the-Amur; Holy Transfiguration in the city of Blagoveshensk, a two-hour flight from Vladivostok; Annunciation in Arsenyev; Visitation in Lesozovodsk; Nativity in Ussurisk; and Our Lady of the Pacific in the easternmost port city of Nahodka, a three-hour drive from Vladivostok.

Not only did Fr. Effing come to serve as a missionary, but he also set out to establish a new religious order, the Canons Regular of Jesus the Lord, which now consists of three priests, including him, as well as several seminarians.

Replanting the Seeds of Christianity

Six years before coming to Russia, he found it necessary to leave the religious order to which he was ordained in 1972 because he felt it was, in his words, "on the skids from liberalism." Teaching in seminary initially attracted him to the Minnesota-based Canons Regular of the Holy Cross, more commonly known as the Crosier Fathers. "My order began to be affected by the false interpretations of Vatican II," he explains, "and weak superiors allowed it to be taken over by unorthodox, modernist members who wanted to remake the Church and the order in their own image, rather than in the image given by Jesus Christ and our founder, Theodore de Celles." Subsequently, the Crosiers had to pay out-of-court settlements for a number of scandals and had to close its seminaries in America.

"I found myself very much in the minority," he says, so much so, "that in the end it was necessary to leave the order. With the closing of the seminaries, I was out of work anyway!"

For six years after he left the Crosiers, he served as rector of Father Duenas Memorial Seminary in Tai, Guam, and then as a university chaplain in the Diocese of Stockton, California. Although he was able to continue his work with students and seminarians, he missed being a part of a religious order. Because he had taken solemn vows and believed in the charism of the Crosiers, he had never *wanted* to leave his order. "I decided to see if I could start a similar order if the old one could not be reformed," he explains. And that's just what he did.

That's also when he ran into new obstacles. His first attempt to begin the new order, which would adopt the same charism as the Crosier Fathers, but follow the discipline of the order in a much stricter way, was in Guam. But opposition from the local clergy there prevented the order from taking root. Next he tried again in California, but ran into the same obstacle: opposition from the local Church. "People just don't like others coming onto their turf," he explains. "So, frankly, we decided to look for a place that had no local clergy, so that there would be no one to oppose such a foundation."

That's when Russia opened up, and the two missions — to re-establish Christianity in the Russian Far East and to found the new order of Canons Regular — looked as if they would work well together. Eleven years later, Fr. Effing and the two other members of his fledgling order are the only priests in Vladivostok, and they have founded almost all the parishes within a thousand miles. "Now I guess *we* are the local clergy," he jests.

Like other orders of the Canons Regular, Fr. Effing's new order follows the Rule of St. Augustine, which includes taking the traditional vows of poverty, chastity, and obedience. A hallmark of the rule is living a life of common prayer in one particular location. "The Cathedral of the Most Holy Mother of God in Vladivostok," Fr. Effing explains, "is a natural place for canons, because there is plenty of opportunity to live, pray, and work together while helping to replant the Christian Faith in this land in which it was almost completely destroyed."

Because Fr. Effing's new order is based upon the charism of the Canons Regular, which emphasizes the common life, he can't live in any other place than the cathedral at Vladivostok. Due to the missionary imperative of his life as a priest in the Russian Far East, however, he or one of his priests visits each of the newly founded parishes at least once a month for Mass, confessions, and baptismal preparations.

To meet the needs of evangelization in such a far-reaching territory, Fr. Effing established an active evangelization program in the Vladivostok parish. "To tell the truth about Christ," he says, "we began a weekly, Saturday-evening prime-time television program that was broadcast to thousands of households in the Russian Far East." Because neither he nor his associate, Fr. Daniel Maurer, spoke Russian when they arrived, the program was initially directed by a layman who had been baptized into a Protestant confession two years earlier. Six months after the Vladivostok parish opened, the program director was received into the Catholic Church.

Fr. Effing's associates have also sent Catholic literature and rosaries to more than seventy-five thousand families all over Russia who live in places where there is no Catholic parish. Several thousand of them have subsequently enrolled in Fr. Effing's twelve-lesson catechetical correspondence course in which they are introduced to the fundamentals of Christianity. This course has now been published on the Internet, helping to catechize Russian speakers in foreign countries around the world.

Fr. Effing also gives three weekly classes in Vladivostok to educate those who would like to become Catholic. He frequently lectures on alcoholism and drug abuse, chastity, Natural Family Planning, and family values at colleges and high schools. All this, he says, is part of the priestly task.

Although not a "missionary priest" in the strict sense, since he was not sent from a foreign country — he was invited by the Russian diocese — he regards the priesthood in general as a mission. "Jesus called the Apostles to follow Him for three years, which was their vocation," he explains. "Then He sent them to preach the gospel, which was their mission. Likewise, priests, after training, are sent on their 'mission.' Each assignment ought to be viewed as a mission."

In the Russian Far East, the missionary quality of his assignment as a priest is acutely evident. Not only did Fr. Effing have to deal with a foreign language and the ill effects of atheistic Communism, but he also had to adjust to cultural differences that presented further obstacles to his work. "I was accustomed to efficiency, democratic methods, and accountability. Those things are not values here," he explains. "Here in Russia, values are more warmly interpersonal, and patience must be the greatest virtue, because here everything moves slowly — except the traffic."

Another cultural difference that presents a grand obstacle is the anti-Catholic hostility that flows freely from the Russian Orthodox Church. In fact, says Fr. Effing, a renewed attempt at repression of Catholicism in Russia has taken hold, this time not by atheists, but by other Christians. This makes the work of evangelization in Russia much more difficult, since the sad division of the Church risks keeping the majority of people who are not members of any confession from taking the message of Christ seriously.

"Since the four dioceses were created in Russia by the Holy Father, the Orthodox Church has sent signals of anger and outrage via the mass media and certain government channels, so that we're meeting all kinds of roadblocks that did not previously exist," Fr. Effing laments. It is often difficult for Catholic organizations to obtain necessary government documents, construction permits, and even simple cooperation. "Even a cafeteria where we had planned to feed children during a catechism camp declined to work with us simply because we were Catholic," he adds.

Before Russia passed a law outlawing mass demonstrations of hate, some Orthodox Russians gathered in protest on occasion at Catholic churches, such as the cathedrals in Novosibirsk and Irkutsk. But it's the *personal* discrimination on the part of some government officials and private individuals with allegiance to the bigotry of the Russian Orthodox Church that is more damaging to Fr. Effing's work in Russia.

Replanting the Seeds of Christianity

"Most of our Orthodox friends who are priests are petrified to have anything to do with us, simply because they fear reprisals from higher up in the Orthodox Church," he explains. "Naturally it's all very sad — not especially because we are suffering, but to see such hatred in the name of Christ and of religion. How I would like to see a happy, healthy Orthodox Church in Russia, but instead it is frightened, revengeful, and not at all attractive, even for Russians at the present time. While they blame Catholics for 'proselytism,' they continue to drive their own people away by the lack of charity and misunderstanding of Christianity on the part of many priests, and even bishops."

Russians who are stirred up by such anti-Roman fervor hold to a centuries-old grudge. "They can't forget the days when Roman Catholicism was the official religion of some of the enemies of Russia in Europe — like Poland," says Fr. Effing. "But I remind them that the Orthodox Church killed more Russian Old Believers than the Inquisition did, not to mention the millions Stalin killed."

Many in the Far East believe that the conversion of Russia will take place, not by the establishment of the Roman Catholic Church across the country, but by the reunion of the Russian Orthodox Church with the Catholic Church. "We pray for a reunion of the churches every day," says Fr. Effing, noting the grave importance of cooperating Christians in this land that has been ravished by antireligious forces. "I love the Orthodox Church and have many Orthodox friends. When can we be really and officially at peace with one another?" he asks.

Besides maintaining his parishes and preaching the gospel, Fr. Effing and his fellow Catholics have been able to accomplish a great deal of charitable work that shows they have the right intention of helping Russia. "Our charitable work is done without regard to religion," he says, "so the greatest number of beneficiaries are, of course, Orthodox." Approximately forty percent of all Russians are at least nominally Orthodox; fewer than one percent are baptized Catholics.

To minister to social needs, Fr. Effing has helped set up numerous programs that provide direct assistance to Russians who have immediate need of health care, food, clothing, and shelter. In 1992, for example, he helped establish a local chapter of the international Catholic relief organization CARITAS. It operates a free medical clinic, a home health-care program, a thrift shop, and programs for children, including street children; it also collects and distributes food.

In 1998 he helped establish the first crisis pregnancy center in Russia. Since child prostitution and abortion are severe problems throughout the country, Fr. Effing saw the need to provide an alternative for the women who believe, mostly for economic reasons, that abortion is the only option for them. In Russia, the first country to legalize abortion, all abortions are provided as a free service of the state, whereas it costs the equivalent of two months' pay to deliver a child. For this reason and others, "the death rate is now much higher than the birth rate," says Fr. Effing. "If this continues, the Russian population will implode with dire circumstances in the years ahead." After being trained by Americans who operate a crisis pregnancy center in Dayton, Ohio, a few of Fr. Effing's parishioners opened the Woman's Support Center in a tiny office in Birthing Hospital #5, the only maternity hospital in the city that did not provide abortions. Since then, eight crisis pregnancy centers have opened in Vladivostok and neighboring cities with the assistance of Fr. Effing and American benefactors.

In addition to the hands-on, in-the-street type of charitable work, Fr. Effing is an officer in four charitable organizations. He is president of the regional CARITAS chapter. He also started The Foundation for the Poorest, where most of the work has been with women prisoners in two states, and for which he was given official recognition by the regional prisons council. He is a board member of the Vladivostok branch of Say No to Alcoholism and Drug Abuse, in which capacity he has given more than ninety talks in Russian public schools and universities about the problems of alcoholism and the treatment of substance abuse. Furthermore, he is the founding pastor of the Parish of the Most Holy Mother of God, which operates charitable programs such as a soup kitchen, a street-children assistance program, and support of a gerontology department at a local hospital.

Although the social work is very important to the Church's activity in Vladivostok, Fr. Effing sees the spiritual work as the most important. The center of any parish community, he says, is the Holy Sacrifice of the Mass and the other sacraments. As a Canon Regular, he places a good deal of emphasis on the Liturgy, which he says is aimed at directing our attention to Jesus in order to be best prepared to receive the sacraments of the Church.

In addition to celebrating Mass each day, one of Fr. Effing's favorite liturgical events of the year is a communal service at the cathedral celebrating the Anointing of the Sick, which takes place annually in late September before the first snow. "Winter can be hard for our elderly, who usually don't have cars or telephones and often live in tall apartment buildings without elevators," he explains. "Even if they can get to public transportation, they still face the daunting task of either climbing the slippery slopes up to our church building from the main street of Vladivostok, or they risk the steep, icy dirt road which comes down to the church from the new Beauty Avenue. Parts of the city never have the snow plowed all winter. Many of the elderly simply can't get to the church in wintertime, so the anointing takes on an even greater meaning for them."

Fr. Effing's work hasn't been accomplished without some sacrifices on his part. The material and cultural sacrifices are obvious, but the most difficult sacrifice the priest has had to make, he says, concerns prayer. "I never realized how difficult one's prayer life becomes when you have to pray in a language not your own," he explains. For his first five years in Russia, almost all of his formal prayer had to be in Russian, which at first he barely understood. "I concentrated on saying it correctly and preaching in Russian. For my older brain to deal with Russian, I had to turn off English completely, so that I couldn't even do private prayer in English. So there was no consolation for me in prayer. It was an important and unexpected result of serving in a foreign country, for which I never had any training."

For twenty years, Fr. Effing had been accustomed to a daily morning hour of prayer and meditation. "After coming to Russia, I had to abandon that," he says, "because I simply could not stay awake for the hour, probably because my brain was trying to deal with a new language. Now I am beginning to manage it again."

Ten years later, after much practice, he can pray freely in either Russian or English. Beyond prayer, his language skills are helpful in other obvious ways. For example, he's now able to lecture effectively in Russian, and as a trained scientist and graduate of Cornell University's premier Astronomy Department, he delivers talks on various topics pertaining to modern science. "The university people in Russia are excited to get to know an educated priest who is a scientist," he says. "They were told by the Communists that only ignorant, uneducated people believe in God."

The topics he teaches on at the universities in Vladivostok, Nakhodka, and elsewhere are not limited to science, of course.

Another of his specialties is speaking on the theory of alcoholism and the treatment of the disease, which is so rampant in Russia. "I think my university and school work — where, according to the laws of Russia, I can't directly proclaim the gospel — is still evangelical work, because faculty and students get impressions about what religion is and what priests are like through hearing me lecture. Often I have contact with students and faculty at a later date when they come to visit us at the parish, to attend concerts, or when they just come to Sunday Mass out of curiosity that I may have aroused in them."

Fr. Effing sees teaching as a major part of his mission as a priest. For most of the years before he arrived in Russia, he taught in high schools, seminaries, and colleges. When he was a teaching assistant in the Astronomy Department at Indiana University, it was the first time in his life that he was directly responsible for teaching students. "I was impressed by the awful responsibility of having to teach others," he says. "I realized that the rest of their lives and perhaps even their eternal lives would be influenced by my teaching and example. It made me stop and think."

For Fr. Effing, the relationship between science and religion was important. Although he understood early on that many scientists, like his teacher Carl Sagan, were ideologically biased against Christianity, and others were simply anti-Catholic, Fr. Effing has always seen science, and especially astronomy, as an aid to understanding the Creator. "Astronomy does give one a sense of wonder which supports one's faith," he says, "and it also deals with some ultimate realities, which is why I thought astronomy was a good subject to be taught in seminary, if any science would be taught there."

"A priest is a teacher," he summarizes, "because Jesus said to 'go forth and teach all nations.'" And, of course, for Fr. Effing, that includes the nation of Russia. His only regret is that he doesn't get to work one-on-one with students more. As the head of the Vladivostok deanery, he answers for a region about as big as California, Washington, and Oregon combined. As pastor, he shepherds five parishes with a combined area about the size of Wisconsin. "I have large distances to cover, and a lot of social work, as well as evangelical and catechetical work, so, for now, I am more directly involved in administration than teaching."

As he hopes to attract more priests to serve in that part of Russia, which Pope John Paul II has called "the end of the earth," he is also hopeful that someday he will again be teaching more. Until then, he's resigned to go where he's needed and to do what must be done.

Chapter 4

The Soldier-Priest

Fr. Patrick Rohen has never been one to shrink from a fight. The forty-five-year-old priest serving in the shadows of the Montana Rockies has always seen his calling, even before he entered the priesthood, as aiding and defending those most in need.

That's one of the reasons military recruiters were begging for his assistance in light of the escalating conflicts around the world in which the United States is involved — in Iraq and Afghanistan especially. The Air Force wanted him. The Navy wanted him. He chose the United States Army. In 2003, at a time when the U.S. military was strapped for Catholic chaplains to minister to American soldiers stationed the world over, Fr. Rohen answered another urgent call — to serve the Military Archdiocese for a period of at least three years. "The Army needs around four hundred priests," he says. "They now have fewer than a hundred."

Why was this priest, serving as pastor of four parishes the size of Delaware in the mountains and prairies of western Montana, such a hot commodity? "A high-ranking Army officer called me up recently and said I had exactly what they're looking for." It was an effective approach, he jokes. "They were looking for someone who was a priest, had already completed military chaplain training, and had extensive experience with pastoral counseling in life-and-death situations."

In the eyes of the U.S. Army, Fr. Patrick Rohen fit the bill. Before he was ordained, he served as an enlisted man, led as an infantry officer, completed military chaplain school, and even served as a military chaplain. On top of all that, the Army was impressed with his past experience in pastoral counseling — an integral part of life as a military chaplain. He has counseled the sexually abused, the spiritually abused, drug addicts, alcoholics, and even child molesters.

At the age of seventeen, on the day after his high school graduation, he began a five-and-a-half-year stint as an enlisted soldier in the U.S. Air Force. His active duty took him to military bases in Texas, Michigan, Arkansas, Oklahoma, Germany, and Italy. Ironically, it was during his time in Italy, stationed at NATO's Aviano Air Force Base, that he became interested in Evangelical Fundamentalism, an "experiment" that would lead him away from the Catholicism of his boyhood for more than a decade.

The year was 1978, the "Year of the Three Popes." Fr. Rohen vividly recalls the death of Pope Paul VI, the election of Cardinal Albino Luciani as the first John Paul, and the new pontiff's unexpected death just thirty-three days later.

"I specifically remember the election of Pope John Paul II," he said. Considering that this Pope has been one of the great heroes of Fr. Rohen's priesthood, he finds it doubly ironic that it was during the year of John Paul II's election to the Chair of Peter that he would be wooed by Evangelicals who rejected the Pope's ministry, as well as many other specifically Catholic doctrines.

"The strain of Protestantism I got involved with didn't overtly hate the Catholic Church," he says. "But there was definitely an 'attitude' toward the Church over there."

One simple reason he was won over to the Evangelicals was that no Catholic chaplaincy was available while he was stationed in a remote part of Italy, right in the heart of Christian Europe, not far from Rome. He attended Christian services and study groups with the Protestant chaplaincy, which he found accommodating to his desire for "the things of God." The other main reason he was swayed by Evangelical Fundamentalism was what he considers his weak education in the Catholic Faith. "It's not that I grew up in a wacky, liberal parish," he explains. "I just simply could have used more solid catechesis. By the late Sixties and early Seventies, things had already begun to unravel in the Church. There was a tendency toward irrelevancy." The transition period instigated by the Second Vatican Council created plenty of confusion, especially in the area of catechetics. "No one seemed quite sure what the Church taught anymore," he says. "The dust had not yet settled."

The fact that no Catholic priest was regularly available during his time in Italy left an indelible mark upon him. "Where was the Church?" he wondered, at a time when he was young, far away from home, and feeling quite alone in the world. "The Evangelical Fundamentalism that I was exposed to seemed to provide answers — answers to spiritual questions."

Rohen subsequently enrolled in Chicago's Moody Bible Institute, the well-known Protestant theological college that has attracted the likes of Dr. James Dobson and the Reverend Billy Graham. Six months after leaving active duty in the Air Force, he enrolled at Moody, at which he earned a Diploma in Theology in 1984.

Thoroughly versed in the Protestant approach to Scripture, Rohen took his fresh theology diploma with him into the Army National Guard. He continued his education at the University of Toledo, where he participated in the Army's ROTC program and received his commission as Army officer. In 1988, he graduated from the University of Toledo with a degree in Human Services. In the late 1980s, he served as an infantry officer in an important leadership position, training troops that were later sent to the Persian Gulf during Operation Desert Storm.

It was around this time that Rohen started feeling drawn back home to the Catholic Church. He was volunteering at an inner-city soup kitchen in Toledo when he made a startling discovery. Almost all those volunteering there, helping to feed the poor, were Catholics. In fact, the soup kitchen was sponsored by St. Francis de Sales Church, a local Catholic parish, which Rohen began frequenting. "I started to see the social-justice dimension to the Catholic Church," he explains. "The Lord used that to lead me back to the Church." He soon found himself learning much more about the corporal works of mercy and was introduced to the spiritual works of mercy as well.

In addition to the social-justice dimension of the Church, Rohen was also attracted to the traditional trappings: the prayers and devotions, the churches, the statues, and other works of devotional art. In short, he sorely missed the sacramentality of the Catholic Church. More than all else, he realized he missed the sacraments, especially Penance and the Eucharist.

In 1989, after eleven years of wandering outside the fold, he was received back into the Catholic Church at St. Francis de Sales Parish, where he found that he was spending quite a lot of his time, both working and praying. Eventually he found himself in the front pew of the church on many days after daily Mass, asking himself whether he was being called to Holy Orders. The answer, he says, turned out to be yes.

Two years later he was enrolled at St. Meinrad's Seminary, in rural southwest Indiana, studying for the priesthood in the Catholic

Church — quite a change, he says, from being a lay student at
Moody Bible Institute. It was during these seminary years that he
also attended the United States Army Chaplain School, the institution that trains the Army's future chaplains. "When I was in the
military," he explains, "I saw a real need there for Catholic chaplains, and with my background, I thought military chaplain school
was where I was called."

In the course of three months at Fort Monmouth and Fort Dix,
Fr. Rohen completed the training program, which included learning about war crimes, military law, how to deal with conscientious
objectors, and how to crawl under machine-gun fire. "In the chaplain school," he explains, "you become a soldier. You get your hair
buzzed. They put boots on you, and you march. The most important part of it all is understanding the need to exert leadership and
developing the skills necessary to lead. That's important to every
single priest, whether he's in the military or not."

Most of the field training, such as how to set up a tent, wear a
gas mask, and use military radios and vehicles, was already familiar
territory for Fr. Rohen. In fact, his previous experience as an infantry officer landed him an assignment as personnel officer. Being an
officer, he explains, carries a great deal of honor and a great deal of
responsibility: "Like priests, officers lead. They are the president's
representatives in certain military matters. That's why they receive the honorary title of Sir or Ma'am. Officers have a lot of authority and power. They make the decisions."

After completing the chaplain program, Fr. Rohen served on
reserve duty as a chaplain candidate in the Ohio National Guard.
"I drove around the state in a Humvee, visiting the weekend warrior camps that were assigned to me," he explains. "My duty was to
provide the soldiers with pastoral and spiritual care, and to counsel the commanders on moral and morale problems."

Priest

For any Catholic military chaplain, he explains, there are two basic groups of people who require pastoral care. First, the chaplain has to take care of the general needs of all soldiers in any particular unit, because more than likely, due to the shortage of military chaplains from every denomination, only one chaplain will be present at any given time. "Sometimes all it takes is being present to the soldiers, checking up on them to see how they're getting along. They're all away from home. They're away from their families, and morale can sink low at times. One of my duties is to provide moral support from the spiritual side of things."

Other times, he says, it's not so simple and straightforward. The military chaplain is never at a loss to exercise his role as pastoral counselor, dealing with personal, moral, or even family issues that affect the spiritual lives of the soldiers: drug and alcohol abuse, sexuality, depression, and issues of social justice, for example.

"The military is having problems like every sector of our society today," he explains, "and they are faced with many of the same challenges. Our soldiers are coming forward out of a narcissistic society, and it's somewhat depressing. Consequently, all branches of the U.S. military need good priests who can provide moral and spiritual guidance. It really comes down to a spiritual problem."

In periods of wartime combat, add to that assisting the soldiers through physical and emotional trauma, taking care of the dead and the dying, counseling prisoners of war, and looking out for the general spiritual warfare of all combatants, even that of the enemy. "We're trained to monitor prisoners of war," explains Fr. Rohen. "When we get into a wartime situation, I have to make sure the prisoners of war are not being killed or tortured. We're taught to monitor according to the standards set forth in the Geneva Convention."

The second group he's responsible for as a chaplain are those who are specifically Catholic — to provide spiritual direction

where necessary, and above all to provide them with the sacraments by hearing confessions and offering the Holy Sacrifice of
the Mass.

During his time as a chaplain in the Ohio National Guard, he
observed that many of the soldiers — some of them almost completely unchurched — were very interested in the spiritual side of
things. "I had to field a lot of questions about the Catholic Faith
especially," he says. Some of the questions were posed to him by
ideologue Protestant apologists who wanted to argue with him,
usually to no positive end. But most, he said, were sincere questions by soldiers who simply wanted to know how Catholics deal
with some of the more difficult questions of our times. "I would get
asked questions like: What if a serial murderer came up to you in
Confession? Why don't Catholics believe in contraception? Or
why doesn't the Church accept divorce when most other denomi-
nations seem to believe it's okay in some instances?"

It was an opportune time to preach the Catholic Faith to a cap-
tive audience and to clear up many of the popular misconceptions
about the Catholic Church held by Protestants, e.g., about Mary,
the role of the Pope, the Holy Sacrifice of the Mass, the sacraments, and the role of Scripture — misconceptions Fr. Rohen experienced first-hand as an Evangelical Fundamentalist.

Fr. Rohen left the military as a First Lieutenant in 1994, nine
years before the military conflicts in Iraq and Afghanistan, when
he would again be called to serve not only the Church, but his
country as well. Where did he expect to be shipped out to? "It's not
the M.A.S.H. days of Fr. Mulcahey, who was assigned to just one
unit," he explains. Since there are now so few chaplains, he ex-
pects to be moved around a lot. "It won't simply be in a hospital. I
could be in an armored cavalry unit, in an air assault unit, or in the
infantry." Chances are, he says, he'll be moved around among all

these, "wherever the Army needs me." That most likely means in the most hostile fighting zones, since it's much more probable for chaplains to be in those areas where fighting is ongoing. Wherever he gets stationed, he'll remain in the thick of things, right alongside the combatant soldiers.

Being a soldier-priest takes a lot of courage. In a sense, it takes a man who is fearless. It takes a "warrior" who isn't the least bit daunted by the prospect of being on a battlefield, facing death — his own and that of others. At the same time, he emphasizes that he's no warmonger. Rare is the chaplain who is, he says. "My spiritual director, a Vietnam Vet, calls me a 'warrior.' That might describe my personality, but I'm also a man of peace" — a peaceful warrior, you might say.

The Just War Theory is something that concerns Fr. Rohen as a Catholic priest and as a military officer. "We must always use the minimum amount of force to achieve our military goals, military strikes should be a last resort, and we must constantly work and pray for peace," he says.

Most people probably don't readily associate compassion and empathy with a warrior, but, says Fr. Rohen, "a Catholic chaplain should be a compassionate man. He must be empathetic, willing and able to put himself in other people's shoes, and say, 'I guess I can see why they feel the way they do.' To give an example, when I work with AIDS patients, I don't necessarily agree with or understand their prior actions, but I can certainly see why they are hurting and why they're upset. It's my duty to offer them the love of Christ and to hear their confessions and get them ready to go be with God."

Compassion and empathy aren't always inborn traits among priests, but they can often be acquired through the more difficult experiences of life. Fr. Rohen has seen people at their worst — in prisons, in mental hospitals, in soup kitchens, and even in his seminary. "I've gone to the places where people have hit rock-bottom." Part of developing empathy is experiencing your own suffering and coming into close contact with the sufferings of others.

In Fr. Rohen's opinion, empathy is one important quality that's sorely lacking among many priests today — in the military, yes, but more so outside the military. "The problem," he explains, "is that many of these priests have never suffered. They are too comfortable, and they are too often unwilling to take a look at their lives. They are not introspective. But when they do go through suffering themselves, they are better able to sit down with others and shepherd them. Unfortunately, today's priests run the risk of being aloof and arrogant — so much so, that it considerably weakens their ministry."

Fr. Rohen has seen his share of suffering in his many and varied experiences with pastoral counseling. "I've dealt with spiritual abuse, sexual abuse, physical abuse, alcohol and drug abuse. I've dealt with priests who were alcoholics." His role as counselor, he emphasizes, is always grounded in a spiritual, moral, or pastoral perspective. "I'm not a psychologist," he says. "I'm not a social worker. I'm a priest."

Typically, he says, when people come to him for counseling, he offers moral support, prays with them, and tries to understand what they need in the way of spiritual direction. But that's not all. Sometimes, especially in cases of abuse, he works closely with a master social worker, a medical doctor, or a clinical psychologist. "I don't just turn them over to anyone, and I don't abandon them," he explains. "I refer them to a practicing Catholic who will understand their Faith, their moral underpinnings, and their religious sensibilities. I take care of the spiritual aspect, and the psychologist or social worker will take care of the affective aspect."

Priest

It's important, says Fr. Rohen, for the priest to have the desire to reach out to those most in need. "We don't need any more Levite priests," he says. "I can't just walk by those who are suffering — no matter who they might be — and figure that someone else will take care of them, or that they'll take care of themselves." This reaching out is a most important aspect of leadership, both in the military and in the priesthood.

Sometimes those "most in need" might be people you literally find repulsive. Nonetheless, says Fr. Rohen, a priest mustn't shirk his duty. One year he worked in the Indiana prison system. There he came into contact with convicted child molesters. He had counseled those who had suffered from sexual abuse. Now he found himself counseling the perpetrators of this evil.

"These people have spiritual needs, too," Fr. Rohen says, "as much as we might not want to admit it." He emphasizes that they ought always to serve out their punishment as anyone convicted of a serious crime, and they need to be kept away from contact with children. "But they're still people, and they need the grace of God. We can't abandon them. I pray with them and offer them the love of God. In order for them to repent and be converted, they have to understand that God still loves them, even though they must atone for their sins. They've got to be given a sense of hope so that they can be properly forgiven. You can't take that away from anybody. There is room for forgiveness for everyone in God's kingdom."

He has also worked with AIDS patients, both men and women, many of whom contracted the deadly illness through homosexual relations. "There's so much involved with AIDS — a sense of shame, rejection, and sometimes abandonment," he says. Many of the AIDS sufferers Fr. Rohen has counseled are also in dire financial straits from overwhelming medical bills.

"If a person comes to me and tells me he's suffering from AIDS," explains Fr. Rohen, "first and foremost I see him as a person made in the image and likeness of God, and I desire to help him or her spiritually. That doesn't mean that I am an enabler. That doesn't mean I tell him it's okay to live a sexually promiscuous lifestyle that does not follow the Church's teachings. It simply means that I treat that person with the love of Christ. I don't tell him he can just go do whatever he wants and feel good about it; but I do treat that individual with the love and respect due to every man and woman."

He has seen some AIDS sufferers repent, develop a deep prayer life, and become exemplary Catholics. "They have come to understand that they will soon face the particular judgment, and they're preparing properly for that — as we all should be doing." Such is the good fruit of attentive pastoral counseling.

Yet of all those whom Fr. Rohen has come into contact with during his priesthood and seminary years — child molesters, AIDS patients, alcoholics, and drug abusers — perhaps the people who most upset him are the religious authorities of our day. His problem is not with authority, but with abuse and neglect by those in positions of authority within the Church — the same problem that Christ Himself faced.

"In His day, you had the Pharisees and the Sadducees," he explains. "The Sadducees were the wealthy, liberal priests who denied the Resurrection. We've got plenty of that type today with wealthy, liberal priests who deny any number of Church doctrines, up to and sometimes even including the Resurrection. On the other hand, there were the Pharisees, who were stuck in a legalistic mode of religion. We've got plenty of pharisaical types today, too."

It doesn't come down to a problem of liberal versus conservative, he says. It comes down to the faithful versus the lazy and uncharitable. "It all comes back to empathy," he says. "As a priest, I've got to be understanding of the situations of others — of everyone. I cannot be lazy and not reach out to them. I cannot be uncharitable to them by telling them they're going to Hell. I cannot give in to moral liberalism and tell them what they're doing is just fine, while helping them feel good about doing whatever it is they might be doing. I must give them the love of Christ, the medicine of Christ, and that means that I must help them understand the teachings of the Catholic Church and assist them in every way possible to accept those teachings and to live by them. To do that, I must have empathy, and I must be a leader."

An important part of being a leader, he says, is fulfilling one's moral obligations. As a pastoral leader, and especially as a priest, Fr. Rohen has found it challenging to fulfill his moral obligations when it comes to dealing with various forms of abuse; but he has never been one to shrink from duty.

Abuse comes in many forms. During the nationwide priestly abuse scandals in 2002, the world was horrified to learn of the extent to which some Catholic priests and bishops were involved in the cover-up of sexual abuse of children. For a variety of reasons, most priests did not or felt they *could not* speak out against these abominable crimes committed by fellow men of the cloth.

Fr. Rohen wasn't one of them. He broke the code of silence. "I felt the moral requirement was greater than the possible consequences of my speaking out. Priests need to stand up and be men," he says.

Fr. Rohen repeatedly spoke out in defense of abused children, and that included saying some things that many in the clergy did not want to hear. Some fellow priests denounced him as "too conservative," a telling indication of how some clergy regard the subject of the burgeoning scandals. His public comments did, however, make him a hero in the eyes of many laypersons, especially those who had been sexually abused as children.

In December 2002, Fr. Rohen told the *Washington Post* that "somebody's got to speak out on this. The whole problem is the world of secrecy and shame. In order to get beyond this denial, in places where cover-ups and incompetence have been demonstrated, those bishops should retire."[2] The priest's words were amplified across the nation when the article was carried on the Associated Press newswire.

Fr. Rohen's words were not idle. Knowing that his comments could lead to serious consequences, a few months earlier he and another priest, Fr. Stephen Stanberry, called for the retirement of Bishops James Hoffman and Robert Donnelly for their handling of cases of alleged clerical sexual abuse of children in his hometown of Toledo, Ohio. Fr. Rohen told the *Toledo Blade:* "Martin Luther King, Jr. had to speak out when people were suffering, and he said this: 'It is always the right time to do the right thing.' The present crisis is so grave that the [two Toledo] bishops should retire immediately. There is no shame in retiring. They should both step down and let Rome bring someone new onto the scene who is more capable of adequately responding to the crisis."[3]

Fr. Rohen doesn't believe he said anything earth-shattering or even extraordinary. Plenty of others didn't look at it that way. "By speaking out," he says, "a lot of people who've been abused said, 'Finally, we have a priest who cares about us.'" People called him at his Montana parish from all over the country just to thank him

---

[2] Pamela Ferdinand and Alan Cooperman, "After One Cardinal Resigns, Catholics Ask: Who's Next?" *Washington Post*, December 23, 2002.

[3] David Yonke, "In the Center of Controversy," *Toledo Blade*, October 19, 2002.

for saying what he did. Their overall sentiment, he explains, was simply that they were glad a priest spoke out. It was as simple as that.

Because he's a Catholic priest, Fr. Rohen's words were nevertheless seen as controversial by some, not the least being his brother priests and bishops. That's because there's an unwritten law that says Catholic priests should not publicly criticize other Catholic priests — a sort of "thin, black line." This type of reasoning, though, is partly to blame for the many problems besieging the Church regarding revelations of scandal: priests and bishops failed to speak out when they had the moral and sometimes legal obligation to do so. "We've got a problem [with clerical sexual abuse of children] that has come about over a period of decades, and it's not going to be fixed with any easy solution. But the first step we have to make is admitting that there's a problem."

Fr. Rohen believes that, above all, children have to be protected — protected in every aspect of their lives, and especially when placed under the auspices of the Church or her representatives. "The protection of children," he says, "is a nonnegotiable moral absolute. Many priests probably do deal with sexual abuse properly, but some just don't know what to do when confronted with this type of problem." Fr. Rohen is speaking of the many instances in which priests have turned a blind eye to brother priests and other Church representatives, lay or religious, who were suspected or known to be abusing children. It's an unconscionable situation, he says.

These words aren't idle ones either. In one of his previous parish assignments, Fr. Rohen found himself facing exactly that type of situation. Members of his parish approached him to allege the sexual abuse of a young boy by two men who held positions of responsibility at that parish.

One of the big questions people have had about the scandals is: Why weren't the police and the child-protection services notified? To understate the case, the fact that common sense and proper procedure were routinely neglected angered not a few good people. "I had to report these alleged child molesters right away. I had to get the authorities involved immediately," he says. "That's the law. The Church is not an investigatory agency, and that includes the bishop's office. If there's even a suspicion of child abuse, we're obliged to notify the authorities immediately, and it's their duty to investigate."

The two suspected men at his parish were later arrested, found guilty, and served time in prison. That means that he protected not only the child who was being sexually abused, but also other children who might suffer similarly at the hands of the two perpetrators. "That's what is paramount," Fr. Rohen emphasizes. At the same time, he was also protecting the Church, since the Church would be held responsible, knowing about suspected child abuse yet doing nothing about it. "Part of the problem over the years is that so many of these cases have simply not been reported — and not just within the Church. All of society has a terrible problem with incest and child sexual abuse." Nevertheless, he says, the Church ought to be setting a good example for society to follow.

"We need to break the whole problem of secrecy and denial in the way we handle these problems," says Fr. Rohen. "Secrecy is not the same thing as confidentiality. Secrecy is dysfunctional. It can sometimes be a real challenge to break those bonds of secrecy, but for priests especially, we are no less than morally obliged to do so."

It's an obligation and a challenge that must be courageously met by more warrior priests, today and in the years to come.

Chapter 5

Fostering Vocations
for Future Generations

Fr. James Gould is best known for being one of the most successful vocations directors in the United States since the Second Vatican Council. For fifteen years, from 1985 until 2000, he was charged with promoting and fostering vocations to the priesthood for the Diocese of Arlington under Bishop John Keating. During that time, the relatively small diocese of sixty-five parishes in northern Virginia produced an average of eight new priests each year. By the year 2000, the average age of priests in Arlington was forty-two — twenty years below the national average! What makes these statistics even more impressive is that this was accomplished during a time of vocations drought throughout much of the Western world.

The formula for his success? "Unswerving allegiance to the Pope and magisterial teaching; perpetual adoration of the Blessed Sacrament in parishes, with an emphasis on praying for vocations; and the strong effort by a significant number of diocesan priests who extend themselves to help young men remain open to the Lord's will in their lives," Fr. Gould says. Quoting Pope Pius XI, he emphasizes that "no matter how we seek, we shall always find ourselves unable to contribute anything greater than to the making of good priests."

Some vocations offices over the past three or four decades have tried to implement complicated programs to attract men to the priesthood. But Fr. Gould took a different approach. There was no "vocations team" involved with the diocese's Office of Vocations while he was director. "Teams tend to be a bureaucratic burden," he explains, "with all sorts of agendas that cost great amounts of money. Simplicity, as much as generosity, is a virtue for vocations directors."

Rather than spending his time with "paper projects," Fr. Gould preferred to travel to parishes to preach about priestly vocations at Sunday Masses, as well as to groups at schools, colleges, scout retreats, Knights of Columbus councils, and even military bases. This, he says, gave him a chance to look into the eyes of parishioners and talk directly to them about fostering and promoting vocations to the priesthood in the Catholic Church.

The Diocese of Arlington set very concrete goals for vocations during his tenure. Each year, he explains, "we looked for ten new priesthood candidates, rather than ten-percent increases. 'Ten men' is a concrete goal, and every priest plays a part in achieving this goal." Only in a couple of years during his time as vocations director did the diocese fall short of that goal. But one year Arlington had *twenty-two* new men entering seminary — more than enough to make up for some of the other years. Consequently, today the Diocese of Arlington has no "priest shortage," as other American dioceses increasingly do.

Fr. Gould also attributes the vocations success in the Arlington Diocese to the presence of the Poor Clares Monastery in Alexandria, where the sisters constantly pray for vocations to the priesthood and religious life. "They are very dear to the heart and soul of the diocese," he says. This spiritual aspect must always be present, he adds, if any success in vocations is to be expected or even hoped for.

Still another reason for success was the presence of two good bishops. First, Bishop Thomas Welch, himself once a seminary rector, judged the success of priests by how effectively Jesus Christ "got across the Potomac River" each Monday morning, a reference to residents of northern Virginia who commuted to work in Washington. Said Fr. Gould of Bishop Welch: "He expected the priests to be men of prayer who could preach with courage, teach with clarity, and serve with charity." It was Bishop Welch, later the Bishop of Allentown, Pennsylvania, who invited the Poor Clares into the diocese. The bishop's goal, he says, was to synthesize the academic, social, and spiritual lives of his parishioners, which was the same goal he had for his seminarians. The second bishop was John Keating, who, says Fr. Gould, actively sought out men who demonstrated prayer, generosity, hard work, and sacrifice. Fr. Gould calls these qualities the "four marks of a vocation" and stresses their importance for priests and seminarians. He was first introduced to the four marks by his uncle, Fr. Dudley Day, an Augustinian priest from Chicago and one-time vocations director for his order.

For the candidate in seminary, prayer comes first. "He has to develop a solid prayer life — going to Mass every day, saying a daily Rosary, and he should pick a saint who is clearly an advocate for him," suggests Fr. Gould, who says that, as a child, he picked St. Joseph — figuring he wasn't busy, since everyone was talking to the Blessed Virgin.

Without prayer, Fr. Gould emphasizes, the ordained priest can't even hope to partake properly in the source and summit of the Catholic priesthood. And that is, of course, the Holy Mass.

"It's the most important part of the day. Every intention I have for each day goes into that Mass. If you're going to represent the Lord *in persona Christi* ['in the person of Christ'], you've got to be able to talk to Him, and you have to want to talk to Him. For the priest, preaching, teaching, and sanctifying is rooted in the Catholic Mass." Prayer is the absolute-bare-minimum prerequisite.

Hard work is the second mark. "I always said I'd like to send every seminarian to a hardware store to work for a summer. In a hardware store, you not only learn the practical skills of plumbing, electricity, and mechanics, but you also learn personalities. You learn about people from those who come in. You learn something about the business world. You interact with people. You're always talking. And you're always service-oriented.

"The greatest malady in the priesthood today," adds Fr. Gould, "is not 'liberals' or 'conservatives.' It's laziness and indifference. In this age of 'collaborative ministry' with the laity, many priests may have slipped away from the meaning of hard work. They don't do house calls. They don't teach CCD. They don't visit the grammar school, and they don't teach RCIA — and that's a problem."

Generosity comes next, he says. "The candidate has to be able to answer the question: What are you going to give these people? That's what generosity involves. I've got that old Irish superstition that says that if you're not generous to people in need, then you're not going to get what *you* need" — and he makes it a point to live by that maxim. "When I was a kid, my father was in a motorcycle accident. During the year and a half that he was out of work, the Gould kids — there were eight of us at the time — weren't able to enjoy a lot of things we normally did." His great aunt, Helen McGonigle, however, made a lasting impression on him by putting up the money for all the children to continue at the Catholic grammar school. Aunt Helen was the true example of the "Catholic single," says Fr. Gould. She worked many hard years for the phone company, never married, and came to live with the Gould family to help "tame the wild beasts in us," he explains. "God bless her, she would chase after us with a belt, broom, or shoe to keep us in line, but every afternoon she would sit and say a Rosary or two, three on a bad day, that we wouldn't be digging ditches one day. Years later, my brother, then a young Marine, and I, a concrete laborer on summer break from the seminary, would call her up exhorting her to start beating the beads as we were digging ditches."

Looking back on those difficult times, Fr. Gould thinks the parish could have cut his parents a little slack on the school tuition, but they didn't do it. Worse, he adds, during the whole time that his father was out of work, the parish priest came to the Gould house only once. "I never forgot that," he says. "I thought that if I was ever a priest, I'd show up a little more often. It's an important aspect of generosity."

In his own priesthood, Fr. Gould has realized the necessity of generosity many times over. One particularly remarkable incident came when he was made pastor of St. Raymond's in Alexandria, Virginia. He was charged with the tremendous task of building a church building, school, and rectory for this recently founded parish. Part of building a new parish from the ground floor up is the daunting and often unpopular task of fundraising. Fr. Gould's task at St. Raymond's was even more daunting than for most priests put into that position. Sadly, his predecessor was discovered to have been embezzling church funds on a rather grand scale and was swiftly dismissed from the diocese. Many Catholics in the parish who had trusted the former pastor to be a good steward of their donations — something they likely expected of any Catholic priest — were crushed.

Priest

In an effort to restore trust in the parish, Fr. Gould was primarily concerned with exercising the virtue of generosity. "I came in and told the parishioners on my second weekend that I was going to give a year's salary to the church building project. And then the next year, after completing the pledge for a year's salary, I called the parish finance committee together and said I was going to give $10,000 over the next five years. After that, the people in the parish came out of nowhere with generosity and raised $2 million almost overnight. Now we've got more than $8 million raised for a $9.2 million project." That's not a bad start in a parish that just two years before was deeply wounded by a ruinous financial scandal.

The virtue of generosity is intimately connected with sacrifice, the last of the four marks of a vocation. Many people think that this should be first, but it should come last, Fr. Gould says. And what exactly should aspiring priests be sacrificing? The first thing that comes to mind for most people is giving up marriage and family life. "Everyone wants to talk about sacrifice first," he adds. "But without prayer, without hard work, without generosity, sacrifice would be meaningless in the life of a priest or anyone else."

Prayer, hard work, generosity, and sacrifice played a significant role in the development of his own vocation, attests Fr. Gould. "Generosity was definitely a hallmark of both my parents and my childhood," he says. He was one of eight children born to James and Alice Gould, and each child was born in a different city, covering eight homes in seven states. His father was a member of the Army Medical Corps and his mother a nurse. The whole family grew up moving wherever they were assigned, so they were no strangers to change. In an obvious display of the virtue of generosity, James and Alice Gould had eight children of their own when they decided to adopt a child from Korea. They had previously attempted to adopt a Vietnamese baby, at the end of the Vietnam War, but one of the U.S.-bound planes carrying the orphans crashed en route, and the adoption program was shut down by the American government. "People would always ask my parents why they wanted to adopt a ninth child when they already had eight," he remembers. "And my dad would always answer: 'We had a fertility problem.'"

Prayer was also an important part of Fr. Gould's upbringing. "We were on our knees every night before we went to bed. Every child said a Hail Mary, and Dad would start with an Our Father, and Mom would end with a Glory Be. We just needed another kid to make it a complete decade."

His parents, he says, explicitly lived out, day to day, the model of prayer, hard work, generosity, and sacrifice. The four marks were active in his family life before they imbued his priesthood. And that points to the wisdom of Fr. Gould's favorite maxim: the true vocations directors are at home, not in the chancery offices. "I was never blind to that fact," he says. "As a vocations director, I always said, I'm just the gatekeeper: I'm the one who helps get them in, and I'm the one who helps throw them out, if need be. But the real vocations directors are the parents.

"If parents want to foster vocations, I counsel them to follow the standards of prayer, hard work, generosity, and sacrifice. It doesn't matter if they go to Mass one day a week or seven days a week — as long as the kids can see that the prayer life of their parents is credible, hard work that is credible, reaching out to kids and expecting things of the kids, then you are going to find vocations coming."

Fr. Gould believes that's why he felt his call to the priesthood as early as the age of seven. He remembers telling his father of his desire for the priesthood in second grade. "My classmates in both grammar school and in high school all knew that I'd be a priest some day. Upon graduation from high school, the school newspaper listed the colleges the students would attend, except for mine. With my name was the word *priesthood.*"

After high school, Fr. Gould did go on to attend Niagara University in Niagara Falls, New York. His years there gave him the opportunity to discern his vocation quietly while studying philosophy, which he knew would help him prepare for studies in seminary. He distinctly remembers one April morning during his junior year there when, after the daily Mass, he walked confidently to the classroom building, picked up the pay phone, and called his mother. Since it was a Tuesday, in the middle of the day, she thought something was wrong, but instead he just told her that "it was time to go."

"Go where?" his mother asked him.

"To seminary," he replied.

There was a long pause on the other end of the phone, and then she said, "I'll tell your father." All those years of quiet expectation erupted in that simple conversation; the cat was out of the bag; the decision had been discovered and made. The moment was comparable to when a young man decides, proposes, and announces marriage.

That phone call was preceded by an equally memorable event. On the previous Christmas vacation, when he was home with his parents, in a reflective moment (if such can be found in a house of nine children), he was looking out the window at an Iowa blizzard when his mother walked into the room.

"What are you thinking about?" she asked.

"I'm thinking about the time when I won't come back here again," he responded. He had no idea why he said that to her just then. He had always planned to come back to Iowa, where his parents had eventually put down roots. At the same time he knew that Iowa just didn't seem like home to him.

Once he had decided to apply for seminary, Gould told the Vincentian priest who was president of the university at the time. Fr. Kenneth Slattery was ecstatic, he remembers. "He didn't try to sign me up for the Vincentians, but he was a great support. And when I would see him in the classroom — he taught ethics — or when I saw him at Mass or anywhere else on campus, he would pull me aside and ask how I was doing. His attention was encouraging. I had a great admiration for Fr. Slattery, as he rejected the state funding from New York, known as the Bundy Money, so that the university would not have to compromise its Catholic identity by taking state funds."

That Easter he returned to Iowa, where he had spent his high school years. "The priests in my home parish there were the real heroes in my life," says Fr. Gould. His pastor, Fr. Charles Phelan, would have teenagers lined up against the wall to go to Confession. "You could go tell Fr. Phelan and confess that you shot your mother or that you robbed the local bank, and he would say, 'Glory be to God you're here. Glad to hear you confess it. That's great.' It didn't matter what sin it was, he would always say, 'Glory be to God.' " The other priest, Fr. Frank Nugent, was his high school religion teacher and his spiritual director, who provided an inspiring role model as a teacher and preacher in the classroom, at the altar, and in the pulpit.

As it turned out, though, Fr. Gould didn't apply for seminary back in Iowa. There was an unsettling thought of a greater need in Virginia. He and his family had once lived in Alexandria, Virginia, in what is now the Diocese of Arlington. He also had several friends who were attending the newly founded Christendom College in Front Royal, Virginia. He stayed with renowned Church historian Professor Warren Carroll when he visited the diocese to take a look around.

He didn't have to go far.

When Fr. Gould went to Mass at the local parish on the first day of his visit, he told the priest there that he was thinking about the priesthood and was looking to apply to seminary the following year. He still remembers being impressed with the enthusiasm of the priest's response. This was more encouragement for his vocation.

Then he went to visit the first priest he had ever known: Msgr. Martin Quinn at Blessed Sacrament Church in Alexandria, where Fr. Gould had attended grammar school for a few years. "I called him up and told him that I was thinking about the priesthood. I explained that I was a student in New York, and that my parents were living in Iowa, but that I had attended Blessed Sacrament grammar school and hadn't been back in thirteen years." So Msgr. Quinn invited him over, sat him down, and fed him a ham sandwich, potato chips, and a soda. He then proceeded to tell the future Fr. Gould everything that had happened in his parish over the past thirteen years, since the Goulds had moved away. "It was like he was my own grandfather," he says. "I even stopped at the old neighborhood and some of the folks treated me as if I had come home from war. They recalled the time my father was teaching me how to ride my first bicycle out on the front walk. I knew I was home."

The upshot of his visit to northern Virginia was that he felt he would be wanted and needed as a priest there. "I had dropped into a diocese where there was obviously a collective interest in vocations," he says. "I happened into a swirling pool of activity for promoting vocations, and Bishop Thomas Welch, who had founded the young diocese, was churning the waters."

Consequently, the Diocese of Arlington is where Fr. Gould stayed. He was sent to St. Charles Borromeo Seminary in Philadelphia and was ordained by Bishop Welch on May 9, 1981.

The question that often comes up for Fr. Gould is "What are you doing *here?*" He answers, "God always seems to put me into places where I didn't expect to be. He placed me in a great family, and I went to great schools, a great college, and a great seminary. I was ordained into a great diocese, serving with heroic priests, and I worked under great bishops."

Bishop John Keating, who succeeded Bishop Welch as the Bishop of Arlington, was another of Fr. Gould's heroes. "He was easy to work for because he always had a great interest in promoting and supporting vocations," he says. And he believes that it's Bishop Keating's prayer, hard work, generosity, and sacrifice that continued to build and maintain the "strong fraternity of priesthood" that Fr. Gould experienced under Bishop Welch.

The four marks of a vocation are manifest in the lives of so many priests in northern Virginia that vocations are encouraged by giving good example. "It's like in business: if you have something good to sell, people will invest in it." And as vocations director, Fr. Gould has long had a vested interest in seeing that he has a good "product to sell" to young men discerning the vocations call.

Another important aspect in the life of any vocations director is the selection process of candidates for the priesthood. Fr. Gould readily admits that for the past four decades, some vocation directors have not faithfully fulfilled their duty in selecting the proper candidates: "Working in vocations is a two-way street. There are candidates to be avoided, and those to be promoted. In the topsy-turvy world of the last four decades, someone switched the street signs. Vice became virtue, and virtue vice."

In fact, there have been plenty of highly suitable good men, he says, who have been turned away simply for embracing the teachings of the Church, especially about the nature of the priesthood and about the more controversial issues of sexual morality. For Fr. Gould, however, acceptance of the Church's teachings is a prerequisite for admission to a seminary as a candidate for the Diocese of Arlington — as any conscientious Catholic would expect.

The interview process is very important, says Fr. Gould: "In interviews with candidates, these are the kinds of questions I would ask: Where are you from? Where did you go to school? What were your grades? Do you have any relatives who are priests or religious? Are your parents still living, and are they supportive of what you are doing? How many siblings do you have? What is your faith background? Do you know any priests?"

"Then I go on to the harder stuff: Have you ever cohabitated with anyone? Are there any kids out there who look like you?

"And then I would say, 'I have to ask you this, and I apologize for having to do it, but what is your sexual attraction?' That's the way I phrased it back in 1985 when I first started interviewing candidates. And almost every guy, about ninety-nine percent of them, would say, 'Father, I understand why you're asking the question,' and they all knew homosexuality in the priesthood and in the seminaries was a problem, even back then. Most of them said no, they weren't homosexual, didn't have same-sex attractions. If they said yes, I had to tell them I couldn't accept them into Arlington."

Back in the mid-Eighties, explains Fr. Gould, one of the diocese's primary concerns was that the gay activists in the Washington, D.C., area might publicly identify gay seminarians or priests. There were, in fact, a couple of incidents around that time in which priests were "outed" by activists in Arlington as a "payback" — presumably for the Church's teachings on homosexuality.

Fr. Gould relates a case in point: a priest in the neighboring Archdiocese of Washington connected with a local Catholic homosexual group was successfully baited by a young gay man who was put up to the task by activists bent on "punishing" James Cardinal Hickey for preventing the formation of a gay club at Georgetown University — which is, of course, a prominent Catholic institution. The activists set up sound equipment and video cameras in an Arlington hotel to expose the priest giving in to his vice. Fr. Gould later met the young man who had baited the gay priest.

"I asked him if he thought this was wrong, if it was immoral, if it was unjust, or if it was sinful. As smooth as silk," relates Fr. Gould, "the man said to me, 'We wanted one' [a priest]. So in those days, the concern was about aggressive homosexual activists going after the candidates."

Fr. Gould admits that this isn't the highest motive for rejecting homosexually inclined candidates to seminary. Yes, it does protect the homosexually inclined young man from later being lured and publicly humiliated by the activist crowd, but, more important, it protects the Church and the diocese from unnecessary scandal. And long before the end of Fr. Gould's fifteen-year tenure, he says, he realized well enough that homosexuals don't belong in all-male, celibate seminaries. "There were a few cases where homosexuals were aggressive after others in the seminary," he remembers, "and had to be dismissed. Some of them would get past me during the interview process, and once or twice we had to dismiss a candidate because of homosexual activity."

It is instructive to note, he adds, that no psychological test proves homosexuality: "You pretty much have to take the candidate's word for it. Most of the time the homosexual's psychiatric profile will say 'narcissistic.' And that's telling. He often exhibits a very strong interest in the self" — something not conducive to the ministry of the priesthood.

"The other thing that will sometimes surprise people," he says, "is that in the American experience, we may find that the active homosexual cleric or seminarian is not always a 'liberal,' that is, with libertine attitudes toward sexuality. He may have a great devotion to the Blessed Mother, as well as other saints. He may sometimes preach or teach some very traditional lines, and yet he practices the homosexual lifestyle on the outside. It is a psychological disorder; that's the only way that I can describe it. To be fair, there are a lot of homosexuals in the ranks who are chaste homosexuals. But with the weakening of the cultural mores, their life in chastity must be extremely difficult."

Sadly, the issue of homosexuality has come to dominate discussion about the priesthood in recent years, especially during the great media blowup in 2002 over clerical sexual abuse of minors. The vast majority of the priests involved in these scandals were self-professed homosexuals who acted out on young men or adolescent boys. "It's more than obvious that homosexuality in the priesthood is a serious problem. It's the elephant in the living room. The Church has reached a point where it can no longer ignore this."

Fr. Gould has been called upon frequently to comment publicly upon the mushrooming scandals in the Catholic Church. In his media appearances, he has said he is careful first to identify properly the different "players" involved in the scandals. He says they fall into four categories: seminarians, sexual offenders, active homosexuals and heterosexuals, and "the average Joe."

Above all, he insists, the Church must be concerned with the seminarians, many of whom will one day be our future Catholic priests. "If we don't identify homosexuals in the seminary as being a serious issue, then we risk continuing to face big problems later on. We've got to make some hard-line decisions at this particular time in history," he says of admitting homosexuals to seminary, a topic that the Vatican has taken up amid the scandal-charged atmosphere in the United States and elsewhere. "The majority of the scandals that have come to light do not involve pedophiles, although the cruel ones you see in the paper do. The majority of the $1.3 billion that was lost on litigation went for homosexual activity and ephebophilia — sexual attraction to post-pubescent minors. It's not an issue of a passion for an individual, which is fleeting. We're talking more about an appetite, a seriously disordered attitude that lingers. So you've got to identify and weed out these candidates from the very beginning, and ask for candidates who are stable in their psychological and mental health, who are in good physical health, and who are free from habitual serious sin, habitual mortal sin."

As an aside, he adds that the one category never identified in the Church abuse scandals regards the number of men who entered the seminary and soon after resigned, within eighteen months, because they were scandalized by the immoral behavior of their fellow candidates or formation leaders, or both.

The second type of "player" of the scandals is the perpetrator, the abusive priest who has slipped through the cracks. This is the type who needs to be dismissed — and swiftly, Fr. Gould says. "There's no room anywhere in the priesthood for a man who sexually abuses minors."

The third group has been more neglected and ignored, and yet needs to be challenged, says Fr. Gould. These are the priests who are sexually active, whether homosexual or heterosexual. It is instructive to note that during the watershed meeting of U.S. bishops held in Dallas during the summer of 2002, the bishops indicated they were interested *only* in cases involving children. "This was tantamount to giving *carte blanche* to all those involved in other lapses in modesty, chastity, and celibacy," he points out. This is dangerous, he says, "because more and more priests feel isolated due to the priest shortage in most areas of the country. He's living alone and nobody seems to notice the behavior and the lifestyle. The Church needs to reach in and go after the pornography on the computers and on the television, after the subtleties of sexuality, because their priests' strength is slipping away in their compromises concerning chastity — and not only chastity, but modesty, too. And we've got to go in and challenge the guys who are completely off the mark. You have to bring them back in line or let them go. The scandals to the innocent ones far exceed keeping the perpetrator or the activist around."

This third group, says Fr. Gould, has to be challenged by a philosophy and agenda that is thoroughly Catholic, and this challenge needs to begin the day each man enters seminary and continue throughout his entire priesthood. It is, in fact, the responsibility of the superiors to see to this. In the priesthood, those who cannot or will not maintain the vow of celibacy need to be identified, investigated, and assigned to a sound therapy program. Failing this, Fr. Gould suggests, they should be suspended. "God knows we can no longer morally or financially afford to ignore or cover up these problems. We need to once again address our concerns to the salvation of the souls of our clergy. It's that important to the mystery and mission of the priesthood."

Fr. Gould is careful to make a distinction between active heterosexual priests and active homosexual priests. The heterosexuals are typically driven by a fleeting passion for an individual woman, he says, while homosexuals are more often driven by a disordered appetite that they seek to satisfy with anyone who can be used, even if it means preying upon the innocent and defenseless. This is a controversial position to take, he knows, but in his experience, the evidence bears out this conclusion. That's why it's important to understand what has come to be known as the "gay subculture" within the Catholic priesthood and among the activist Catholic laity. As with all subcultures, those within them tend to "promote their own" while discriminating against those who don't support their particular agenda. In the case of a gay subculture, Fr. Gould says, it only follows that this exacerbates the problem.

The fourth group consists of what Fr. Gould calls the "average Joe," the priest who works diligently, hears confessions, says Mass, prays his Rosary, and tries to promote the correct teachings of the Church. "If you don't go after the third group," he warns, "don't be surprised to find that members of the fourth group are going to wobble into the third group. Because they're going to reason that it really doesn't seem to matter much anymore."

To acknowledge that there is a problem within the ranks of the priesthood requires faith and morals. "Wherever there's a faith problem, there's a moral problem. Wherever there's a moral problem, there's a faith problem. That's a rule of the confessional," says Fr. Gould. "The two always walk hand in hand." And that points to the accompanying problem of dissent. Dissent from the teachings and disciplines of the Catholic Church is an issue that's directly related to the moral problem. That has to be openly recognized by everyone in the Church, he stresses.

After all, he adds, the duty of a priest is to raise people to a higher standard of holiness, to enhance the consciences of all — believers and nonbelievers — to understand that virtues will always attract and vices will always divide. "We're called to save souls, and we should never lose sight of that." And, despite all obstacles, Fr. Gould is very optimistic about the future of the Catholic priesthood in the United States. In every era there have been problems in the priesthood; but these problems, as serious as they sometimes have been, have always been overcome by the grace of God and with fidelity and obedience to God's will by clergy and laity alike.

It's no different now, Fr. Gould believes, as long as we don't fall prey to denial, one of the worst enemies of the priesthood and the Catholic Church in recent times. Only by facing these problems head-on can we maintain a solid, healthy priesthood. Fr. Gould's life is proof positive of that.

Chapter 6

Overcoming Opposition
from Within and Without

Fr. Eduard Perrone remembers aspiring to be a priest in his early grammar-school days, but by the time the ambitious Detroit native reached junior high, he had pretty much abandoned the idea in favor of a career as a professional musician. But even in his music, he was never far from the heart of the Church. In fact, it was in part the Church's traditional liturgical music that later inspired him to return to his childhood aspirations.

Music was a family love and even a family business for the Perrones. Eduard's father, Philip, was a trumpeter and owned a music store when young Eduard was a boy. His mother, Maria, played piano, the instrument he grew up playing and loving. In high school, he studied music at Cass Technical, a centralized public school in downtown Detroit, an institution that would now be called a magnet school. "Any student who excelled in one discipline could attend Cass and consort with other kids who were gung-ho on a subject or a career," he explains. "It made for a great feeling of solidarity and healthy competition with high standards."

At the same time, the young Perrone was intimately involved at his parish, St. Clare of Montefalco in Grosse Pointe, just outside the Detroit city limits. "I served as an altar boy and sang in the choir. Being involved in music was just natural for me," Fr. Perrone says. From eighth grade through high school, he also attended the Palestrina Institute, a music program offered by the Detroit Archdiocese. "It was exceptional," he says of the five-year program. It was at the Palestrina Institute that Fr. Perrone first took courses in music theory, harmony, and ear training. He learned choral singing, Gregorian chant, organ, and piano. "It was tremendous," he recalls. "They turned out generations of talented church musicians." Sadly, the institute closed a few years after Fr. Perrone graduated from high school in 1966.

From there, he continued his pursuit of a career as a musician. He received a scholarship from the University of Louisville and continued his study of piano and composition, receiving a degree in Music Theory and Composition. As he did at Cass Tech, Fr. Perrone continued playing in an orchestra at college and remained involved in Church music, playing scores from great Church musicians such as Bach and Mozart.

He first seriously felt his call to the priesthood during his senior year at Louisville. "I remember," says Fr. Perrone, "it was like a revelation. It was a totally uninvited and unreflective thought. I remember thinking, 'I know what I'm going to do. I'm going to be a priest.' It was in the evening just before I went to bed, and the thought filled me with such happiness. It was something I hadn't considered in years. It came to me, and I slept so well that night. But when I woke up in the morning, I said to myself, 'Wasn't that a stupid idea I had?' But something happened there that night."

The Catholic Church in those years was undergoing tremendous changes, many of them not for the better. Fr. Perrone views that time as a period of trial for many Catholics, himself included. Dissent challenged many people's faith, usually under the guise of making the Church more "relevant" to the modern world. "In a way, it seemed a very exciting time," Fr. Perrone remembers. "There was something new each week."

In the realm of Church music, however, Fr. Perrone greatly missed the use of Latin and Gregorian chant in the Mass, even though he was composing his own liturgical music at the time. He found the folksy "guitar Masses" of the time an embarrassment, and he began to lose touch with the traditions of the Church while he was away in Louisville. Nevertheless, he says, "I was in the best position because I had training in the background of music and the Church, and in Catholic culture generally. I went through that period of tremendous change without losing my faith or abandoning my principles or my cultural heritage."

To this day, Fr. Perrone still gives thanks for his excellent Catholic education and upbringing. The nuns who ran his grammar school and the Augustinian fathers who ran his parish were great influences on him. "Along with my parents, they instilled in me a real love for the Church," he says. "When you're a kid, you really drink it all in."

After college, Perrone returned to Detroit and landed a church job playing the organ, but the parish was awful, he says, and the experience of working there likewise. Then he moved to Old St. Mary's in Detroit's popular Greektown, where the parish offered Mass in Latin. "That was an important bridge for me," he says. "It's a great downtown church run by the Holy Ghost Fathers. I started a music program there, and that was really a turning point for me. It was here that I witnessed traditional Catholicism in action. I saw the devotion of the people, and that really brought it together for me."

It was the influence of Old St. Mary's that brought Perrone to the point of signing up for classes at Sacred Heart, the local seminary, as a lay student. "I decided I wanted to try it out," he says. "I thought I'd just try it out at first by taking some theology courses," he says, "because if I didn't want to stay, I wanted to get out with impunity."

All went well at Sacred Heart that year, and Perrone decided to take the plunge. His first move was to tell his parents about his interest in entering the seminary. "They didn't receive the news altogether favorably, I'd have to say," remembers Perrone. "But they didn't oppose me. They had hopes of me doing something in music. My mother cried, but that doesn't mean anything in particular. My dad thought the way to go was to be a family man. He told me that. He didn't try to discourage me. He just said, 'For me, this is the life, having a family.' My dad was just a very loving family man. Family meant everything to him. My dad was always very religious, but he didn't see how you could live without a family. Even so, he did end up supporting my decision, and eventually he became very proud that his son became a priest."

Fr. Perrone remembers the day when his uncle, who was skeptical of his nephew's calling, helped him move into St. John's Seminary in Plymouth, Michigan. "He said, 'I don't know why we're doing this, because you are going to be out of here in a couple of months.'" But Perrone stayed, although he admits he was often tempted to leave the school because of the "liberal experience" he had there, which he characterizes with one adjective: horrible.

Oddly enough, it was a "street bum" from Greektown who helped Perrone along his way during those difficult seminary days. "Here was a guy who was shabbily dressed and smelled awful," Fr. Perrone says of Nick Psihas. "He was a heavy cigar smoker, and it was obvious that he wasn't in the habit of showering."

Psihas came into Old St. Mary's one day when Perrone still worked there as music director. "He said he wanted to audition for the choir, and after taking a look and sniff of him, I thought, 'Egad!' " When Perrone asked him what he could sing, Psihas began to rattle off Italian opera arias — much to Perrone's disbelief.

"You can sing all that?"

"I can," Psihas responded, explaining that he had once sung in the Met choir, which sounded like a tall tale at first, but Perrone later confirmed that this was in fact true. "He sang in a big basso voice," he remembers, "and he knew all these arias from memory. I was astounded. He was great."

Over the next few years, a friendship developed between the two men. Psihas was born a Greek Orthodox and was raised in Detroit's Greektown. He converted to Roman Catholicism during his college days as a philosophy student of Charles de Koninck at Lavalle University in Quebec. According to Fr. Perrone, Psihas was educated in the philosophy of St. Thomas Aquinas, "unadulterated by modern Thomism." It was from studying Aquinas that Psihas converted to Catholicism. "This guy could quote for me, chapter and verse in Latin, just about anything Aquinas ever wrote," he said of Psihas. "He converted by the light of the Catholic Faith as illuminated by Thomas. I remember him saying to me that the Greeks don't have the truth. Only the Catholics do."

Such sentiments didn't endear Psihas to his family. In fact, once he converted, his family effectively disowned him, considering him to be a traitor to his religious and cultural heritage. "He was rejected outright," recalls Perrone. Emotional problems ensued, and Psihas wandered around from apartment to apartment. By the time he met Perrone, he was on disability, suffered from severe depression at times, and more or less lived on the streets of Detroit until he died some few years later.

Oddly enough, however, Nick Psihas was the one man who helped Perrone see his studies through during his seminary years at both Sacred Heart and St. John's. "I would get together with Nick from time to time," he remembers, "and we had some great conversations. I would tell him what books they had me reading in my courses, theology texts from Protestant thinkers such as Tillich, Barth, and like minds. He told me this was junk and always had suggestions as to what I ought to read to counteract these non-Catholic authors. We had long discussions about theology, and I learned quite a lot from him, a 'simple bum' off the street."

One of the most memorable conversations he had with Psihas, remembers Fr. Perrone, was when the Greek convert let him in on what he called his little secret. It turned out to be the Blessed Virgin Mary. "He told me that I'd never be a good priest unless I have a devotion to the Mother of God, because she's the Seat of Wisdom.

"Now this guy was a Greek, so he wasn't speaking from mere piety or any sentimental attachment. He firmly believed that without the Virgin Mary, I could not fully follow her Son as a priest. He said that with Mary you'll have wisdom and virtue — and he wasn't talking about just any sort of devotion; he meant explicit, authentic devotion to the Blessed Virgin Mary.

"Here was this Greek layman preaching to me with fervor about the Virgin Mary and the theology of St. Thomas. He had such an incredible passion for truth. And even though most people considered him nothing more than a common street bum, he was perfectly lucid and always had incisive commentary on contemporary issues. He had a brilliant mind and was the most outstanding influence on me during my seminary years."

Psihas also encouraged Fr. Perrone to read St. Alphonsus Liguori, who wrote a popular book on the priesthood called *Dignity and Duties of the Priest*. Along with St. Louis de Monfort's *True Devotion to Mary*, Psihas gave Perrone St. Alphonsus's book saying,

"This will cement our friendship." The main message of both books, which Fr. Perrone turns back to each year, is that a priest's duties must be carried out with purity of intention and diligence, and that he himself should strive to be irreproachable in his conduct and manner — a man of prayer. Liguori's book also made plain to Perrone the terrible consequences of a priest who is unfaithful to the grace he is given by virtue of his ordination. "Those two books are still in the back of my mind," says Fr. Perrone, "and still play a big part in my priesthood. The role of Mary, which I promote — and I'm privileged to be presently assigned to a Marian shrine — has made a tremendous positive impact on my life as a priest."

As fate would have it, Nick Psihas didn't live to see Perrone ordained in May 1978 and assigned a few weeks later to St. Peter's Church in Mount Clemens. It took no more than a matter of months before Fr. Perrone experienced the infighting that he has become so used to since that time.

Shortly after he arrived at St. Peter's as a newly ordained priest, his pastor asked him to take over the parish's religious-education program, both the Catholic grade school and the CCD program. "I was eager for anything," Fr. Perrone recalls his enthusiasm as a young priest. "The first thing I did at the school was give a test to all the eighth graders, both in the school and in the CCD program. It was a test about the most fundamental aspects of Christianity and the Catholic Faith."

He was a little surprised to find that many of the students didn't even know that Jesus was divine, others had no idea what the sacraments were, and some had not been to Confession even once in their lives. Fr. Perrone compiled the results and followed up by interviewing all the religion teachers in the school. "When I made my report to the parish religious-education commission," he recalls,

"I told them the whole program had to be scrapped. It was a failure to our kids. And I set out to design a whole new Catholic education program."

Although the pastor supported him, not everyone was happy. "The liberals were in control of the school at that time," he explains, "and I got a lot of opposition. The pastor knew the program was a failure and had recruited me to clean it up. My zeal for priestly involvement allowed me to tackle it head-on."

But once Fr. Perrone concluded that the program needed to be scrapped, some teachers wanted to tackle *him*. "One day at a school Mass," remembers Perrone, "I announced the new program and presented all the religion teachers with a Miraculous Medal. One woman took the medal and threw it across the church in a rage. That shook me up a little, I'll have to admit. I was almost right out of seminary at that time and wasn't yet used to that sort of thing."

But that wasn't the end of the matter. Some of the teachers were unwilling to accept the new program, which emphasized authentic Church teaching that wasn't dumbed-down. Some of the teachers who opposed the young priest took the matter to the Archdiocese of Detroit, and Fr. Perrone was called down to the chancery to explain himself.

The teachers at St. Peter's had complained to the archdiocese that Fr. Perrone was contravening archdiocesan directives. He had written his own catechism books because, as he explains, "the good ones were not on the approved list of textbooks promoted by the Archdiocese of Detroit." In fact, the textbooks he was interested in using in the school were on a sort of blacklist. "So I wrote my own," says Fr. Perrone, "thinking this way they couldn't say I was offending any of their policies."

The protesting teachers collected Fr. Perrone's books and sent them downtown for evaluation by the archdiocese. The priest who reviewed the books found them "unsuitable" for use in the classroom and gave Fr. Perrone a theological critique of his program, enumerating numerous "errors." Fr. Perrone, in turn, sent the critique of his work to Jesuit theologian Fr. John Hardon, who was residing in Detroit at that time. Fr. Hardon, says Fr. Perrone, agreed with him that it was the archdiocesan critique that was loaded with errors. As it turned out, the priest who critiqued Fr. Perrone's books was later laicized and now faces criminal charges for sexual abuse.

"When they wanted to scrap my program, I took my attorney down to see them. I told them they were violating my rights, because they wanted to keep me from teaching the Catholic Faith. Once they saw the attorney, they were just beside themselves."

That was the beginning of what Fr. Perrone calls his exile. In his opinion, the archdiocese was doing all it could to minimize his impact on the Catholics of Detroit. While the decision about the new religious-education program at St. Peter's was still up in the air, he was transferred to St. Genevieve in Livonia.

Fr. Perrone remembers Fr. Ferdinand Wolber, the pastor at St. Genevieve, as a great priest and former military man, who was both orthodox and outspoken. "He'd get up in that pulpit, and the church would just thunder with his voice." One day, soon after Fr. Perrone arrived at the parish, he remembers one of the auxiliary bishops in Detroit coming to the parish for a Confirmation Mass. "Fr. Wolber chewed him out so bad," he says, "for what the archdiocese was doing against my religious-education program." Fr. Perrone had become *persona non grata* downtown.

The run-ins with archdiocesan bureaucrats didn't end there. While an associate pastor at St. Genevieve's, Fr. Perrone organized a pro-life prayer group of college students who met at the parish once a week to pray the Rosary for an end to abortion. "I announced that we'd meet on a Wednesday afternoon from 5:30 to 6:00. It wasn't a social club or anything; we were just getting together to pray."

Much to his surprise, the group attracted twenty students each week. "From that group came the suggestion that we do some more pro-life work. When they told me they wanted to picket abortion clinics, I just about fell over. There's a beautiful Dominican principle that says 'The active life is the overflow of the contemplative life.' So from the prayer group came this movement.

"We didn't really know how to go about doing it," he admits. "I used to read about priests like Fr. Paul Marx going out there and doing this sort of thing. I thought to myself, 'What are we going to do out there in public, standing on the street, carrying signs?' But we did it, and it was quite an experience. We went out to the clinic a couple of times each week, and we'd pray the Rosary out there, walking along the sidewalk."

This was back in the early 1980s, before the practice of sidewalk counseling became popular. "We handed out anti-abortion literature," he says, "because none of the counseling techniques that are used so effectively today had been developed yet. And the result of this was a lawsuit brought against our group by the abortion clinic, claiming that we were trying to shut down their business."

Although the case was taken to court, the abortion clinic eventually dropped the lawsuit, but not without making some news in Detroit. "When the lawsuit hit the papers, Cardinal Szoka called me down to his office to inquire about my sidewalk pro-life activities. I think he was afraid of a lawsuit against the archdiocese."

That case underlined an issue that has long concerned Fr. Perrone: the lack of support that many priests feel throughout their ministry. "There are a lot of young men out there," he says, "who sense that in many places around the country there's a certain lack of solidarity in the priesthood, and I think that sometimes discourages them from answering the call they feel."

To those men Fr. Perrone always offers the same bit of advice: "The need has never been greater in modern times for good priests," he explains. "The priest shortage is acute in too many places, and yes, we need good men who are not afraid to preach the teachings of Jesus Christ. We need good men who are willing to oppose the secular world that is invading the Church. And that sometimes means that they will have to stand alone.

"I try to appeal to a young man's sense of dedication and idealism. This is a time for fighters. There's a battle out there, and if you're a wimp, you're not going to cut it. That's all the more reason to want to be a priest. All the same, just like a soldier in combat, they've got to be prepared for battle, because if they're doing their job, they will invariably get some scars. They're going to find themselves opposing *people* — not only the world, the flesh, and the Devil; they're also going to be fighting forces within the Church that want to subvert Church doctrine and structure. If they believe in the priesthood, and all that our holy Faith stands for, they've got to be prepared to fight the battles."

Fr. Perrone makes a comparison to the September 11 tragedy: "When our country is attacked, all of a sudden our patriotism swells. You get men wanting to join the armed forces, and that's natural. That's how it ought to be in the Catholic Church, too, because we're under attack. The difficulty in our case is that the enemy is on the inside often enough. There's that lack of solidarity. Priests often don't have others backing them. We often don't have that *esprit de corps*."

For that reason alone, the priesthood is a serious challenge in today's Church, but the open culture wars, Fr. Perrone says, are indeed attracting men who want to take up the Cross and answer the call, understanding that they will need to rise to the great challenge of the priesthood.

Sometimes, he points out, certain "persecutions" can work to the priest's advantage through the grace of God. In his own case, when the time came for the archdiocese to give Fr. Perrone his first assignment as a pastor, he was "sent out to pasture," to a parish in rural Capac. Such an assignment is often regarded in clerical culture as the lowest rung on the pastorate ladder. But for Fr. Perrone, it was a source of great blessing.

"St. Nicholas Church was just about as far away from Detroit as possible in the archdiocese," he says. "The parish had very few families, and I would have very little influence beyond my parish boundaries, but I loved it."

In the farm community of Capac, he was able to put to use his many talents that had lain dormant during his previous three assignments as an associate pastor. "When I was ordained, I figured I had to abandon music. I gave it up pretty much except for playing the piano. When I got to St. Nicholas, I immediately saw that my new parish needed some help in the Church music department. We were too small to afford a music director, so I formed a choir and trained them to sing Latin chants. It went over very well and was a beautiful addition to the Sunday Masses."

Fr. Perrone also undertook a church restoration project. The church was small, but it had fallen victim to some of the fashionable alterations of the 1970s. "We were able to completely restore the church," says Fr. Perrone. "We refinished some solid-oak pews that had been discarded from another church and put in a new marble altar to replace the temporary wooden table that was being used. We painted the whitewashed statues, built a bell tower and choir loft, and even installed a beautiful pipe organ. It was like a little cathedral out in the country. It was very nice, and the parishioners were very supportive. I would have stayed there forever, if asked to."

In 1994, however, Fr. Perrone received an unexpected phone call from Adam Cardinal Maida. Departing from customary procedure, the Detroit cardinal placed the call personally, asking Fr. Perrone to take over as pastor of Assumption Grotto in the heart of urban Detroit, a far cry from little Capac. Cardinal Maida explained to Fr. Perrone that he had been highly recommended by the retiring pastor, Msgr. Clifford Sawher, to take over and carry on the unique ministry of this historical parish. Fr. Perrone had served the parish as an associate a few years earlier in the 1980s. So he was familiar — and impressed — with the parish's reputation as a "bastion of orthodoxy" with a strong emphasis on the liturgical and devotional traditions of the Church.

"I was surprised and honored to receive a personal call from the cardinal asking me to take over at the Grotto," he explains. "I was very happy in my previous assignment at St. Nicholas, but I figured that if the cardinal was personally asking me — rather than simply receiving the assignment through the priest personnel board, as is customary — then it was God's will, so I didn't even question it, even though I knew leaving my old parish would be painful."

Catholic culture and tradition is something that greatly interests Grotto parishioners. Even a cursory glance at the parish reveals as much. Gregorian chant, Mass in Latin, reverence, solemnity, and devotion are all staples of life at Assumption Grotto, which is also a popular Marian shrine. "It's not exactly your run-of-the-mill parish," Fr. Perrone comments. "It's a unique place in many ways. It's both historical, founded in 1832, and extremely active, especially for a city parish in a neighborhood that is unfortunately home to very few Catholics."

Assumption Grotto is also unique because the parish attracts its parishioners from well outside parish boundaries. Some travel from as far away as Ann Arbor, Toledo, Saginaw, and even Ontario. "People come here because they elect to come here. We have very few Catholics living in our neighborhood," he said of Detroit's northeast side. It was once a heavily Catholic area populated by German and Italian immigrants until the blockbusting of the late 1960s destroyed most ethnic communities in Detroit, paving the way for so-called "white flight" into the suburbs.

For that reason, according to Fr. Perrone, Assumption Grotto has one of the most active Legion of Mary programs in the state of Michigan. "That's because we've got a lot of work to do," explains Fr. Perrone, who takes the task of evangelization to heart. "Our neighbors are very receptive to the parish. We have almost no opposition to speak of, even among the Baptists in the area, who aren't supposed to be so friendly to Catholics."

The majority of neighborhood residents are what Fr. Perrone calls the unchurched. They're receptive to the Catholic Church and even to priests. "They are perhaps more respectful of the priesthood than some Catholics," he comments, "and it's very difficult to evangelize. Very difficult. But we haven't thrown in the towel yet. We're still at it, and we do what we know we're obliged to do."

Once the Catholics moved out of city parishes in Detroit, John Cardinal Dearden gave his permission for Catholics to cross parish boundaries when choosing where they wanted to attend Mass. That paved the way for parishes such as Assumption Grotto. There's a particular appeal about the parish that has drawn Catholics from all over the archdiocese and beyond. "They come partly because we make it a point to be a teaching parish," explains Fr. Perrone. "We teach the Catholic Faith in all its fullness, preserve the liturgical heritage of the Church, and that generates a whole lot of solidarity among the parishioners who find both solace and encouragement by banding together at Grotto. We don't have the kind of internecine battling that's so common at many parishes today."

In other words, you won't find power disputes between so-called liberals and conservatives at Assumption Grotto. That's due in part to Fr. Perrone's manner of administration. "I tend to be someone who wants to oversee everything," he says. "That's frowned upon today as micromanagement. I don't mean that I do everything, but I have everyone account to me for anything that goes on in the parish." This may be an important point, because there's unity in a parish if the leadership is strong. "As far as the running and organization of the parish is concerned," Fr. Perrone continues, "everything has to come by me. There's a certain efficiency in that. I can make a swift decision, and I don't have to go through endless numbers of meetings and committees."

Nevertheless, Fr. Perrone recognizes that he has his limitations, just like everybody else. "I do operate with the principle of subsidiarity in mind. I expect everyone to do his own job, whether it's maintenance or teaching or playing the organ, but they are all directly accountable to me. We have only one parish committee in which we review finances and parochial activity. Other than that, we have various parish clubs that are social things, and I don't mind saying that we have a good time. We've got solidarity."

It's that fraternal solidarity that's so attractive to many young Catholic families who are committed to the Church and who strive to rear their children in the Catholic Faith, imbuing them from infancy with a sense of the sacred and the divine. One subgroup among them are the homeschoolers, who comprise about one hundred of the eight hundred registered families at Grotto.

Attending Sunday Mass at the parish, one is struck by the number of young families in attendance, many of them with six or more children. "It's not a contracepting community," boasts Fr. Perrone. That's due partly to the fact that he preaches frequently and openly against contraception and abortion. "If you have no pro-life doctrine," Fr. Perrone explains his simple philosophy on the matter, "then you have no people. And we have to have a population.

"It's both physically and morally destructive not to be pro-life. Contraception is a moral deprivation, so I emphasize the importance of remaining in the state of grace and keeping God's moral laws. It's a dominant theme. And that includes talking about sin and Confession, the necessity of the sacraments and daily prayer. None of those are side issues at this parish."

Each Wednesday the homeschooling families meet in the old school building. "We offer various classes that require a particular expertise, such as Latin, drama, music, and computer skills. It affords the students and their families an opportunity to pray, play, study, and eat together on a regular basis, and serves to build an even greater sense of Catholic fraternity and community support."

One byproduct of this type of fraternity is the number of young men from the parish who have entered seminary. Several parishioners have joined the Canons Regular of the Holy Cross, an ancient European order revived by Pope Paul VI. The Holy Cross priests reside at the parish and assist Fr. Perrone with Masses and confessions throughout the week. Some parishioners are students at the Detroit seminary, while others are studying for religious orders and other dioceses out of state. The healthy number of vocations, believes Fr. Perrone, is a testament to the success of embracing and teaching the full truth of Catholicism in the parish.

Indeed, many lay Catholics have been troubled for decades by the lack of catechesis offered in their parishes. Perhaps more of them have lamented the dumbing-down of the liturgical practices since the rebellious Sixties. That's another attraction of Assumption Grotto. Since he arrived at the parish, Fr. Perrone has been faithfully committed to maintaining and promoting the liturgical and devotional traditions of the Church. His background in Latin, liturgy, and sacred music happens to be perfectly suited to the task.

One of the four Sunday Masses each week is sung in Latin, the traditional liturgical language of the universal Church. Because Fr. Perrone is a trained musician — both a pianist and a composer — the tradition of sacred music gets much emphasis. In fact, he himself conducts an orchestral Mass once each month.

Fr. Perrone rejoices over the fact that he is able to continue his music at Assumption Grotto, where parishioners are especially interested. "I'm able to use all my background here," he says of Grotto. "I can bring up this generation with Latin and Gregorian chant and educate them in the doctrines of the Church — all of which play into Catholic culture, which is so important to those who have sought out Grotto parish." "Respect for Tradition and love of the saints," is his unofficial motto there.

"It seems that all the things I loved about architecture, history, and music, as well as the wisdom of the Fathers — so much of what I identified with as being Roman Catholic — I could now 'crank up' as pastor at Grotto. Ordinary people come here, and they say, 'This is Catholicism; this is Tradition; this is what the Church has always been doing.' That's been so exciting and gratifying."

Many often wonder what is the underlying root of Fr. Perrone's successes at Assumption Grotto. The answer to that, he says, is simple: prayer. For most people, three a.m. is the middle of the night. Not so for Fr. Perrone. Three a.m. means "top o' the morning" to him.

"When I get up at four, I almost feel like the whole day is shot," he says, half-kidding. For the past twenty-five years, Fr. Perrone has risen at this ungodly hour to begin his day in prayer. Before celebrating Mass each day, he prays his Rosary, keeps a Holy Hour before the Blessed Sacrament, exercises at the school gym, showers, eats breakfast, and prays Morning Prayer (Lauds) in the church with parishioners, all before 7:30, when he celebrates the daily Mass at Grotto.

The rest of his day, he says, is often consumed with the "busy work" required to keep the parish running soundly. "If all I ever did was attend to the mundane things in the life of a priest, I'd be in pretty low spirits," he explains. For Fr. Perrone, prayer is the foundation for his life as a priest. "Without a solid prayer life, without commitment to personal prayer to Jesus Christ, I couldn't function properly as a priest."

In addition to being a diocesan priest in the Archdiocese of Detroit, Fr. Perrone is privileged to be a Third Order Discalced Carmelite and serves as chaplain to their local community. The heart of the Carmelite vocation, he explains, is contemplative prayer. That's why he was drawn to the Carmelite spirituality. "Every day we're committed to spending at least a half-hour in contemplative prayer. And it makes all the difference in the world. If I don't make contact with Christ a priority — no matter what else I may have to do that day — then I would be lost. Contemplative prayer is my source of strength."

The crises that arise in the lives of many priests stem, he suggests, from a failure to commit themselves to a solid prayer life. Too many priests in recent decades have submitted to the temptations to either become too active or to seek creature comforts that promote laziness. Both temptations seek to strangle the contemplative life. "You can't be identified with Christ without spending the time in being in union with Him through daily prayer. It just doesn't work."

Belonging to the Carmelites also provides Fr. Perrone with the added benefit of community. "There's strength in belonging to a spiritual community like the Carmelites," he explains. The group meets at Fr. Perrone's parish once a month. They pray the Liturgy of the Hours together and celebrate Mass. Fr. Perrone, as spiritual director, gives a spiritual talk, and they get training in the Carmelite life by studying the great works of St. Teresa, St. John of the Cross, and other Carmelite saints.

"Carmel is an effective life of communion with God. It's not centered on battling with the world as an Ignatius would do, although it does encompass an apostolate. It's not a Benedictine life specifically focused on liturgy, although it includes that, because we place an emphasis on the Mass and Liturgy of the Hours. Carmel also has spiritual doctrine, so it's something like Dominican life, but the heart of the Carmelite spirituality is one's personal relationship with Christ and the Church as God present in the soul. Our main emphasis is that God lives in your soul when you are in sanctifying grace. It's a distinct way of life, and the Carmelite authors point the way."

Fr. Perrone's involvement with the Carmelites has profoundly affected not only his personal prayer life, but his preaching as well. Consequently, he believes that an association with a third order is not only healthful for diocesan priests, but also extremely helpful. These communities and similar confraternities were once very popular with diocesan priests in the United States. Many had these associations even as seminarians before they were ordained. With the breakdown of seminary life that followed the Second Vatican Council, most seminarians haven't been exposed to the advantages of such spiritual associations. "But that's starting to change," observes Fr. Perrone, much encouraged by the current crop of seminarians he knows. "Seminarians today seem much less naive about the Catholic Church than when I went to seminary in the 1970s. They might not be more knowledgeable, but at least they appear to be more disposed toward the Tradition and Catholic truth than in my day."

Fr. Perrone returns again and again to that Dominican principle that says that the active life will be a natural overflowing of the contemplative life. That spiritual life, the life of a priest, he insists, must be thoroughly grounded in prayer. Only then will the active, public life of a priest — his ministry — be truly effective. Prayer, he says, is the greatest thing. But then again, he says as much about the priesthood in general: "It's the greatest thing for those to whom it is given. I can't imagine doing anything else."

Chapter 7

Fidelity, Poverty, and Simplicity

Francisco was riding home from work one night when he was mugged by a street gang. They wanted his bike. With little warning, one of the gang stuck a revolver into his ribs and shot Francisco through the chest. The gang stole the bicycle and left the twenty-six-year-old for dead on the crime- and poverty-ridden streets of Cali, Colombia.

The gunman's bullet cut through Francisco's chest and came right out the other side, puncturing his right lung. To his own amazement, he hadn't been shot dead. When he regained consciousness in the hospital, the doctor told him that the bullet — miraculously — had traveled between his aorta and his heart, just missing both. If the gun had not been placed directly against his rib cage, added the doctor, the "wobble effect" from the bullet would have undoubtedly killed him. Francisco was lucky to be alive.

A year before that incident, in 2001, Fr. William H. Hinds first made Francisco's acquaintance in Colombia. Francisco had been a college seminarian from 1995 to 1998 and was considering continuing his seminary studies. Fr. Hinds was on one of his many visits to the Archdiocese of Cali, where he directs the work of

Mission Share, a U.S.-based Catholic charity that, among other things, assists in building churches in the poorest areas of Cali.

"Francisco told me he would like to come to the U.S. and study to become a priest," Fr. Hinds remembers. When the priest returned to his parish in Maysville, Kentucky, the two kept up an e-mail correspondence for several months. "I was, more or less, discouraging him from coming to the U.S. at the time," explains Fr. Hinds. "I thought he should stay and serve the Church in Colombia, where he is needed much more than he is in the U.S."

Suddenly the e-mails from Francisco stopped coming, and Fr. Hinds just assumed that Francisco had lost interest in pursuing the priesthood in the United States. "Then I found out he was in the hospital with a collapsed lung," he says. "I found out from the chancellor of the archdiocese that he'd been shot."

Once recuperated, Francisco was able to testify in court against his would-be murderer, who was subsequently sent to prison. But the rest of the gang vowed to wreak vengeance on the man who sent one of their brothers to prison. The gang put out a contract against Francisco, intending to hunt him and kill him.

Francisco began hiding out, but life soon became intolerable under those circumstances. The gang kept threatening him through members of his family until he finally decided to flee the country. With the assistance of Fr. Hinds, Francisco was able to come to the United States on a religious worker visa in 2002 and today works at St. Patrick's Church, helping the priest with the Spanish-language apostolate there. Still discerning the priesthood, Francisco lives at St. Patrick's rectory and helps prepare the Mexican migrant workers for Baptism, Confirmation, and First Communion. He also coaches the parish soccer team and assists in running a language lab at the school that helps teach the Spanish-speaking children how to read, write, and speak English.

Fidelity, Poverty, and Simplicity

Over the past five or six years, the Mexican population of the Maysville area has been steadily increasing. Fr. Hinds, as pastor, has tried to accommodate them through a Spanish apostolate that assists them both spiritually and materially. The fifty-nine-year-old priest has the benefit of being able to read Spanish and speak it fluently. He attended a college in Lima, Peru, as a Jesuit scholastic and later enrolled in a graduate program in South American studies at Columbia University in New York City. His background is ideal for working with a Spanish-speaking migrant population of both Catholics and non-Catholics who are in great need. Fr. Hinds, who is very respected in the Maysville community, has acted as advocate, social provider, and pastor to them.

First, he offers a Mass in Spanish every Sunday evening — the hub around which his ministry to Spanish-speaking migrant workers is based. He follows the Spanish Mass each week with a fellowship dinner. "There is no middle-class Spanish community around here," he explains. The Spanish speakers are often in a fairly needy position. The weekly Mass and dinner not only feeds them spiritually and materially, but also brings the entire Spanish-speaking community together regularly. They also get a wonderful meal.

Fr. Hinds has proved to be an advocate for them many times. One night, for example, the priest received a phone call from Ricardo. He was in jail. "I found out that Ricardo had been arrested when he was getting into his car, which he had borrowed from someone," he explains. "He hadn't left the parking lot when a policeman approached and asked to see his driver's license. Since Ricardo is an undocumented alien, he didn't have a U.S. driver's license. The car was impounded, and he was thrown in jail on $1,000 bail."

Fr. Hinds sent someone from the parish to bail out Ricardo, who had no one else to assist him. "Most of the migrant workers in the area are undocumented aliens; many are in the same position as Ricardo. They live on farms in trailers or in old houses on the property of the farmers who hired them. They do demanding physical work in the tobacco fields that no one else wants to do. No one else in this society wants to endure the physical hardships of this kind of manual labor; but these Mexicans *want* to do the work, they need the work, and they work hard at what they do. The Mexican workers are here, and it's my job to minister to them."

Of course, he doesn't want illegal immigrants committing crimes any more than he wants his other parishioners to do so. "If we're talking about a drunk driver, for example, I want him in jail, not on the street running me down," he explains. "But if one of the Mexican workers is driving home quietly at night after work doing a job that no one else will do, a man who is sending money back home to feed his children in a country that doesn't have a job for him, I don't think we want to stop him and throw him in jail."

Fr. Hinds readily admits that he has "aggressive social concerns" that are unpopular with some people, even "good Catholics." While it has become common over the past forty years for priests to neglect their priestly ministry to act as social workers, counselors, or social advocates, Fr. Hinds has never lost sight of his ministry, nor has he shirked orthodoxy. He's no social worker. He understands his role as pastor, and his understanding is that he must be concerned with the welfare of his flock, above all their spiritual and moral welfare. Furthermore, he stridently adheres to the teachings of the Church and the proper norms for administering the sacraments. In Fr. Hinds, the Church has a priest whose orthodoxy complements his aggressive social concern — a well-balanced priestly ministry.

Fr. Hinds laments the fact that, in his view, many Catholics who consider themselves orthodox — that is, believing in what

the Church teaches without equivocation — lack any social concerns. "My favorite story about the Catholic Church in the twentieth century," he explains, "is about the future Pope John XXIII
when he was a papal nuncio in Turkey during World War II. Some
Catholics and Jews were attempting to escape Nazi Germany by
heading east through Turkey. So Cardinal Roncalli went around
to the Catholic pastors and asked them if they would help set up
what we would call an underground railroad throughout Turkey,
to help the refugees escape to safety. To his great disappoint-
ment, many of them said no, they didn't want to get involved.
Most of these people were priests with perfect theology and considered themselves 'good Catholics.' But it was just not in their
hearts to reach out to those refugees, people who were at the time
in great need.

"Consequently, the papal nuncio had to talk to the atheistic
mayor, the Communist policeman, the Protestant minister, and so
forth, and a lot of them agreed to help. Only then was Cardinal
Roncalli able to put together a network of support. But then the
question is: What was missing in the person who holds to a flawless
theology, but didn't have the moral courage in the time of crisis?"

Fr. Hinds believes that one of the noble intentions Pope John
XXIII had in mind when he convened the Second Vatican Council in 1962 was combining — in practice — orthodoxy (or what
Fr. Hinds calls "flawless theology") with social concern. "It isn't
enough that you have all the right answers from the books. You
also have to reach out and help people who are in need. In that
way, we can learn something from the world. We can learn from
those who have moral courage and a sense of love for people in
need, despite their deficit in understanding God and the gospel."

Fr. Hinds's goal for his priesthood is "to have a correct theology,
but not to lack on the human side of reaching out to do the things

for our neighbors that ought to be done for them, whether they are Catholics or not."

In his capacity as director of Mission Share, he carries out the task of combining orthodoxy with aggressive social concern by helping the Archdiocese of Cali in Colombia build churches, rectories, and other buildings to house much-needed Church ministries. Cali, he says, "is perhaps the most troubled city in the world." It has long been home to some of the famous drug cartels that have terrorized the nation. Coupled with a civil war involving multi-sided guerilla armies, raging for nearly four decades, and intense poverty of the kind not seen even in the poorest parts of the U.S., Cali is a city in dire need. The work of Mission Share is carried out in answer to Pope John Paul II's call for the people of the United States to better serve their poorer neighbors to the south. "We are working toward peace as Jesus might," says Fr. Hinds, "feeding and clothing the poor, housing widows and orphans, providing dignified places of worship for the impoverished, and supporting proper community development."

The fact that eighty Americans have been taken hostage in Colombia by narco-terrorists, leftist guerillas, and right-wing militia groups over the past decade has not deterred Fr. Hinds from visiting Cali twice a year to carry out his important ministry with Mission Share. According to a travel advisory issued by the U.S. Department of State that warns Americans not to travel to the Andean nation, "there is a greater risk of being kidnapped in Colombia than in any other country in the world." According to statistics gathered by the BBC, more than three thousand people are kidnapped in Colombia each year.

No one in Colombia seems to have any immunity to the terrorism. Not even priests, nuns, and bishops have been spared. In fact, some prominent members of the influential Catholic Church in

Colombia have been targets for abductions and murders in recent years.

To give an indication of the kind of social turmoil of the country, Fr. Hinds recalls his stays on occasion at the house of Cali's Archbishop Isaías Duarte. "He had guards with machine guns guarding the front door," he says. In March 2002, the archbishop was assassinated by two revolutionary guerillas who gunned him down in a poor neighborhood of Cali after he had officiated over a marriage ceremony for 102 couples. Archbishop Duarte had made many enemies in his quest to bring peace to Cali. He had the kind of moral courage that Fr. Hinds speaks of.

Known popularly as the "Apostle for Peace," the archbishop had been one of the most stalwart critics of the anti-Christian elements in Colombian society, often blunt and harsh in his condemnations of the perpetrators of Colombia's violence. He spoke out equally against the leftist rebels and the right-wing militias who have been responsible for thousands of kidnappings and murders, including the murder of two bishops and thirty-seven priests. Just weeks before his murder, he also condemned congressional candidates who bought votes with money from drug traffickers.

"Cali is a most tragic kind of place," says Fr. Hinds.

The main mission of the Kentucky priest's charity is to build dignified churches, priest houses, and parish centers in the most impoverished neighborhoods in and around Colombia's third-largest city. Working directly with the Archdiocese of Cali, Mission Share helped the late Archbishop Duarte to establish forty-five parishes in some of the poorest slums in all of South America. Replacing the ramshackle bamboo huts that passed for parish churches, Mission Share has funded and overseen the construction of twenty-two beautiful and functional church buildings. It has also assisted with building parish schools and rectories, as well as helped to make much needed renovations and repairs to existing buildings. Just last year Fr. Hinds oversaw the rebuilding of the church and rectory for Nuestra Señora de los Remedios in the rural town of Dagua, after rebel fighting had bombed the parish. "Mission Share," says Fr. Hinds, "has been very helpful to the archdiocese in providing much needed infrastructure in what is quite possibly the most troubled city in the world."

None of the parishes assisted by his charity, he added, can afford to build proper churches. "The average income of a parish in Cali is $85 per week, and the people in the parishes that I work with have incomes much lower than even that." Residents in the areas served by Mission Share typically live in one- or two-room tenements built of concrete block or bamboo frames covered by wooden boards. Others eke out an existence as squatters in abodes lacking the basic conveniences of plumbing and electricity, or they simply live in the streets.

Speaking of the churches, Fr. Hinds says that not just any plans will do. "We have three main requirements for the churches we design and build," he explains. "First, the tabernacle must be visible to the entire congregation. In most cases, that means it will be situated in the sanctuary. Second, there must be a spacious use of property, and third, there has to be ventilation."

While Americans have been spending millions of dollars on what many regard as ugly and dysfunctional churches over the past several decades, Mission Share has built more than forty churches in one of the poorest places on earth at a cost of merely $100,000 each. And no one has complained, assures Fr. Hinds, that these churches are either ugly or dysfunctional.

The new churches are all simple but elegant and dignified structures for Mass and devotions. The new buildings also serve as centers of community activity, where none existed before. The result is solidarity and Christian pride that spills out into the neighborhood. "Because a new beautiful church building makes people feel proud about their community," he adds, "residents often react by taking more pride in their own houses and property, fixing up their yards and cleaning up the streets. This reflects the order of the church building."

Another aspect of Mission Share is caring for the numerous street people of Cali. To that end, Fr. Hinds has assisted the work of *Samaitanos de la calle*, the Samaritans of the Street. The Samaritans are a group of approximately three hundred professionals who venture out into the caldron of drug addicts and homeless people each week in the poorest and roughest areas of town. Every Tuesday night, the Samaritans can be seen walking the slums of Cali, providing these people with bread, water, coffee, and milk. The Samaritans also operate two *Casas*, one to feed the poor and the other to function as a drop-in center where the homeless can get clothes, showers, and haircuts. "We also have a dormitory for women and children under six," he adds.

"The Church in Colombia," comments Fr. Hinds, "is the greatest hope for peace, stability, and happiness of the people. Mission Share has enabled Catholics in North America to help offer some of that hope."

In much the same way as he helps Mission Share carry out its work, Fr. Hinds' primary duty as a priest over the past seven years has been as pastor of St. Patrick's Church in Maysville, a small town on the Ohio River amid tobacco fields and pastures. "A pastor is a way of being a priest," he explains. "Not only do I do the things of offering the sacraments in a way that is appropriate so the people can receive them with devotion and understanding, but the life of this community is also my concern, especially the Catholics, but *everyone* in the jurisdictional parish of Maysville."

Priest

Fr. Hinds is always concerned with the ethical issues of the community and the individuals therein, but his particular angle of interest is their spiritual and moral lives. "There's nothing that isn't really of interest to me about the people's lives here: what they're doing, how they're living, and how they work, who's suffering, and who's doing okay."

When Fr. Hinds arrived at St. Patrick's Church in 1995, he took over a parish that had been wracked by scandals for the better part of the previous three decades. "The parish has suffered from a lot of abuse," he says. He knew little when he arrived but later discovered that four priests who had served at St. Patrick's had sexually abused parishioners. One of these priests was a convicted serial child molester who is now serving out a life sentence in federal prison. On top of that, the previous pastor had left the priesthood.

"I didn't come to my new parish in the best of circumstances," Fr. Hinds explains. "On top of that, I am the first priest who is the *only* priest to serve the parish." One of his first goals was to restore the faith of his parishioners in the Church. "I knew enough about the scandals that had occurred. I told parishioners in my first homily that I didn't expect them to trust me just because I'm a priest. I told them I only expected them to believe that my Mass was valid. I wanted them to trust me because they found me trustworthy, not by virtue of my ordination. I expected that I would have to earn their respect. I didn't take it for granted."

He also told parishioners not to expect him to do anything more than what a priest ought to do. "I don't go to parishioners' houses regularly. I'm not best friends with anybody at the parish. There are no kids who are my 'friends.' There never were when I was a teacher, and there aren't now." He admits, however, that there are always some people in a parish who need more help, such as Maysville's migrant workers. I'm closer to some of the Mexicans," he explains, "because they need more, and they come to me more. I get more calls from the jailhouse from Mexicans than Americans. I get more calls from the hospital from Mexicans, too. That's because they have fewer resources, and there's a kind of bond that forms because of that."

A priest has to be all things to all people, says Fr. Hinds, and that's no easy task even in the best of circumstances. "I've never been a believer that the priest ought to be friends with certain people in the parish to the exclusion of others. It happens too often, and I think it's horrible. It's not my job to cultivate particular friendships among my parishioners. I'm expected to serve them all. If someone's child is sick, you'll find me at his home with him and his family because the child is sick, but I make it a point not to accept social invitations from parishioners. I try to keep my ministry as pastor in perspective by focusing on those things a pastor ought to be doing: administering the sacraments, teaching and preaching, and guiding parishioners to fulfill their Christian duties as laymen in the Church."

The culture of priestly abuse wasn't the only problem Fr. Hinds faced when he arrived in Maysville. St. Patrick's historical church building was in disrepair, and the parish school, one of the few that serves grades 1 through 12, had outgrown its facilities. Two temporary trailer buildings, the church basement, and the old rectory building housed ten overflow classrooms. "In order to survive, we had to build an addition to the school, which would cost the parish $3.2 million," he explains, "but I didn't think we could do that until we fixed up the church. It needed lots of work. The idea was that we needed to motivate the folks to make the church look nice and build the school."

Although fundraising — even for projects of necessity — is never an easy task, Fr. Hinds raised the money, restored the church, and built a beautiful new school building for the parish's 250 to 300 students. Part of the church restoration project included the thorny issue of tabernacle placement. When Fr. Hinds arrived, he found that the Holy Eucharist was being reserved at the side of the church. (The tabernacle had originally been designed into the high altar at the center of the sanctuary.)

"I felt that the tabernacle needed to be returned to its place of honor at the center of sanctuary, and that's exactly what we did." Such a move may seem a small matter to some, but, says Fr. Hinds, it was part of returning a sense of the sacred to the church, and with that comes respect and reverence for the Mass and holy things.

Fr. Hinds holds a strong belief that the Liturgy ought to be celebrated according to the norms carefully laid out by the Church. Too often abused by those trying to remake the Mass in their own image over the past forty years, the Liturgy is an outward manifestation of the Church and the belief of the people. The Liturgy, then, must be accorded the utmost respect.

One of the more obvious ways that Fr. Hinds has put his avowed orthodoxy into practice was by complying with a simple document issued by the Vatican and approved by Pope John Paul II in 1997: the official instruction entitled *Ecclesiae de Mysterio: On Certain Questions Regarding the Collaboration of the Lay Faithful in the Sacred Ministry of Priests*. Fr. Hinds informed his parishioners at Sunday Mass one weekend that, in light of the Vatican directives, he planned to make a few changes regarding the distribution of Holy Communion. The document, he says, "clearly requires that extraordinary ministers of the Eucharist should be used in only two situations: to carry Holy Communion to some of the sick, and to assist the ordained in extraordinary situations at Mass. They are not to be used ordinarily at Holy Mass, as a matter of course or habit."

Fr. Hinds explained the document and his decisions to parishioners, whom he felt understood well. "I had waited many months
for specific comments from the bishop," he told parishioners, "but
when they did not come, I felt compelled to act on my conscience.
I did not make this decision because I personally thought the Vatican policy was better than the current American habit of regular
use of extraordinary ministers, but because I felt an obligation in
obedience."

Fr. Hinds felt that his personal opinion was beside the point. "I
think a clear command has been given by the competent authority, and I should comply," he says. Since implementing the changes,
he now distributes Holy Communion himself, or with the help of
the deacon if he is present. If there is a large congregation, as at a
typical Sunday Mass, they both distribute the Hosts; if the congregation is small, the deacon sometimes offers the Chalice. On extraordinary feasts, he adds, extraordinary ministers are used. Since
the changes, Fr. Hinds and the deacon are also the only ones who
go to the tabernacle to remove or reserve the sacred Hosts. Again,
this may seem a minor point to many, but, says Fr. Hinds, it is truly
an important point that has helped restore Catholic understanding of the Holy Eucharist, an essential aspect of our Faith.

Fr. Hinds explained in a homily that Holy Communion is full
and complete whether one receives the Host alone, or the Host
and the Chalice. He had found that before this there was considerable confusion about this particular point, and the meaning and
proper reception of Holy Communion in general.

"I feel that our extraordinary ministers have been reverent and
appropriate in their service in the past. Many have expressed a fit-
ting humility concerning their service and would not want to act
in a way that the Church does not desire. I assured them that their
service has been honorable and devout, and now we have clear

directives which instruct us in the proper roles we are each to play," he says.

Fr. Hinds reports that parishioners at St. Patrick's reacted uniformly with "calm and peaceful cooperation" with his decision. "I felt they understood my thought process, my respect for them, and my sense of pastoral duty. Some agreed with the document, and some did not, but that never became an issue in this situation."

After just a few months of following the new policy, he says, he felt a heightened sense of reverence at Communion time. "How much of this is from our obedience and how much is from the policy itself, I don't know," he admits. "I myself feel the unique nature of the ordained as the one who touches and brings the Lord to the faithful in this Most Holy Sacrament. The clarity achieved by the directives highlights the profound drama of the sacrament of Holy Orders." The great mystery here, adds Fr. Hinds, is not the particular format for distribution of Holy Communion, but the Sacrament itself. Our Lord is personally present to us in a most intimate way to lead us to fulfillment in Him. This great mystery comes via the Church, which deserves our most attentive obedience.

Fidelity to Church teaching and Church norms is an important concern to Fr. Hinds, not only in the celebration of Mass, but also in matters pertaining to the education of the parish's children, especially at St. Patrick's School. When he first arrived, he recalls, the school needed "a lot of direction." He set out from the very beginning to give the school proper direction based on fidelity to Jesus Christ and His Church, and he says that trying to keep the school stable has been perhaps the biggest part of his life over the past six years. "Schools are a tremendous challenge," he says. "To lead a group in a school is very difficult."

During his first few years at the parish, he taught some of the religion courses until he was satisfied that he had a successful and faithful program in place led by teachers who shared his orthodoxy and his love for the Church. "This is really the bare-minimum requirement of any Catholic school," he says.

Just as Fr. Hinds' background is specifically suited to minister to a Spanish-speaking population, it's also suited to meeting the challenging demands of running a school. Before he was assigned to St. Patrick's, Fr. Hinds taught religion and drama full-time at Newport Catholic High School for seven years. Much to his surprise he was assigned there during his second year out of seminary. He quickly became known not only for his refreshingly outspokenness, but also for his theatrical plays. A high school and college actor himself, Fr. Hinds directed and produced seven annual plays at the school.

"The bishop needed someone at the school because it had a problem there with a priest who had been sexually abusing boys just a few years before," he explains. "The diocese wanted to maintain the presence of a priest at the school, so I was assigned there to take over the position that had gone vacant." As in Maysville, Fr. Hinds was called in to lead the community back to faith and trust in the Church.

This scenario is playing out all around the country. The bad example of some priests, he says, has caused a deep wound that needs to be healed. Fr. Hinds finds that, in every case, the formula begins with fidelity to the Church. Again, beyond orthodoxy, moral courage is necessary to reach out to those most in need, whatever the situation may be.

Doing what is right as a priest — following Church directives or insisting on fidelity to Church teaching in religious-education programs, for example — is not always going to be popular with everyone. Too many times, says Fr. Hinds, "I can sense that people are really frustrated with me. Some are upset that they didn't get their way. Other times, maybe I didn't make the right, prudential judgment." The good thing or bad thing about Maysville — depending on how you look at it — says Fr. Hinds, "is that it's small enough a city that I see most of my parishioners every week. In a bigger city, you can be tempted to just say, 'Oh well, they're upset. Too bad,' and you needn't worry much about ever seeing them again. But if I have some disagreement with a parishioner here in Maysville, we're invariably going to have to keep seeing one another on a regular basis. That means it's best to work things out up front as soon as possible and to the best end possible."

On the whole, he says, Maysville is a fairly traditional place, a small city where people seem to appreciate the leadership of someone like Fr. Hinds, who is committed to maintaining a faithfully run parish. "I think there are a lot of people in Maysville who are very glad that I am a priest here. I can feel that," he says. "This is a pretty traditional community, and I fit in well with what they're looking for. Most of the people like it traditional, and those few ideological foes I might have already realize that they're not going to convert me to a liberal churchman so that I'll accommodate their every whim."

Once we drift away from fidelity to the Church, and once we lose our moral courage to reach out to those in need, explains Fr. Hinds, we pave the way for scandal. "This is the cause of much of the recent and not-so-recent scandals we've been hearing about involving priests especially," he says. Sometimes this loss of fidelity and moral courage is due to the modern lifestyle of the diocesan priest. "Position, lifestyle, and comfort," he says, "nice cars, nice meals, nice clothes, nice houses, hobnobbing with the elite, having the best — all this is part of the problem with priests today, and it's nothing new. I think if priests were not so overly concerned with creature comforts afforded to every middle-class American, then the problem of priestly sexual abuse would be negligible or nonexistent."

Part of the solution to the priest abuse problem, Fr. Hinds believes, is recruiting the right kind of men to begin with. "Men are either attracted to the challenge of the priesthood or they are attracted to comfort. We've got to weed out the guys who are attracted to comfort, and we've got to nurture the men who are attracted to the challenge. At the same time, we've got to be careful about the latter group, because some are interested in the challenge in order to attain personal power. On top of all this, we need to recruit men who are willing to embrace poverty. I've never seen a priest who loves poverty and simplicity fall into the grave evils of child abuse and active homosexuality. It's extremely difficult to be spiritually poor if you are not materially poor and simple in your way of life. Poverty is the key toward faithfulness and keeping to the right path."

In addition to embracing poverty, candidates to the priesthood must be chaste, he says. "Just as a man shouldn't enter a seminary until he's ready to embrace the teachings of the Church, I don't really think a man should enter a seminary until he's been chaste for a considerable time." This is just another aspect of fidelity, he adds. "Fidelity is not just essential; it's the bare-minimum requirement for a man seeking to enter the life of the priesthood."

Chapter 8

Spiritual Direction in Scandal-Ridden Times

"It's been a horrible week," the priest had to admit. A tragic problem had arisen: the father of one of his parishioners had fallen and broken his neck. "They now have to decide with him whether or not to continue the respirator. He's paralyzed from the neck down," explains Fr. Timothy Vaverek, one of three brothers from San Marcos, Texas, who all serve the Church as Catholic priests.

Tragedy is necessarily a part of life for a priest, especially when he serves as a pastor. He shares not only in the many joys of his parishioners, but also in the inevitable tragedies, heartaches, and misfortunes that befall them. The mother who came home one day to find her troubled son hanging by the neck from a tree in her backyard, the parents who discovered their middle-aged son lying dead on the sofa, the family who lost a sixteen-year-old boy to a car accident — the forty-four-year-old Fr. Vaverek is no stranger to these tragedies, and as pastor of the 550-family St. Joseph Church in Bellmead, Texas, he has had his share of horrible weeks.

It's the pastor's duty, says Fr. Vaverek, to share in the lives of his parishioners, in good times and in bad, in sickness and in health. "There's the difficulty of trying to be there for people at the time you're supposed to be there — and," he laments, "not always knowing when that moment is."

But even in times of great struggle and grief, the duty of a Catholic pastor is not all suffering and misery. Sorrowful experiences can also be particularly joyful ones. One notable example, he offers, is assisting a parishioner and his family at the time of death, a common experience for a priest charged with the pastoral care of 1,400 Catholics. At any given time, he knows that he has a dozen or so parishioners who could be within a month or two of death. In this case, a priest's first obligation is to assist the dying person to entrust himself to God's merciful love and to make an act of loving penitence.

"A vital part of this process, if at all possible," Fr. Vaverek explains, "is to hear the person's confession, give the apostolic blessing for the dying, confer the Sacrament of the Sick, and give Holy Communion as Viaticum ('the pilgrim's food') so the person may be strengthened by sacramental communion with the Lord for the final journey and the particular judgment that is at hand."

Naturally, he adds, all this is a consolation to the family, and the priest seeks to help family members see the coming death in the light of Christian faith, hope, and love. Often enough, the mere presence of the priest goes a long way toward creating this perspective. It's one of the great things about being a priest, Fr. Vaverek attests. "No one at the deathbed cares who you are, just that you are a priest. An immediate and deep rapport is established when they see the Roman collar. They are happy simply that the priest — ultimately that Christ and the Church — is present."

The rituals for the dying — the Rosary, the litany of the saints, and the sacraments, with accompanying prayers — give the family and the dying person a way to pray and to express the profundity of the moment spontaneously. Fr. Vaverek says that often priests will find a patient thought to be comatose or not "with it" suddenly make the Sign of the Cross or begin to mouth the Our Father or the Hail Mary! These are deeply moving moments for everyone.

"I am always struck by the rites when I make the prayer of commendation: 'Go forth, O Christian soul, in the name of God the almighty Father, who created you, in the name of Jesus Christ, Son of the living God, who suffered for you, in the name of the Holy Spirit, who was poured out upon you. . . .' Far from fearing death, we command the faithful Christian, as it were, to go that he may be at 'home with God in Zion, with Mary, the virgin Mother of God, with Joseph, and all the angels and saints.' "

Thus, dying a Christian death is not so much a moment of sorrow and grief, but a time of tremendous joy — true Christian joy that is rooted in the theological virtues of faith, hope, and love. The priest shares in that great joy, of course, not only at the moment of death, but also at the time of birth, that is, the spiritual birth conferred upon each new Christian he baptizes in the name of the Father, and of the Son, and of the Holy Spirit.

"Certainly it is always a joy to baptize a baby," notes Fr. Vaverek. But the single most memorable aspect of his last ten years as pastor of St. Joseph's — "the thing that I hope will weigh for me on the Last Day," he remarks hopefully — are the children who are being born in his parish; children who, without his influence, would not have been born.

"I have parishioners who have reversed their sterilizations. I have parishioners in tricky financial and health circumstances, but who prudently have had babies to a point that it is a bit of a joke in the parish," he explains. And why this baby boom in Bellmead? Precisely because of Fr. Vaverek's clear preaching on the nature of human sexuality, marriage, and the family as taught by the Catholic Church and particularly emphasized during the long pontificate of John Paul II.

The births of babies are concrete results in which a priest can take particular satisfaction. "I have caused many babies to be born in a spiritual sort of way," he says gratefully without a hint of boast. Priests — much the same as doctors, teachers, or architects, who typically have more tangible products — sometimes pride themselves on what they deem accomplishments. "We might say, 'I did this good, and I did that good.' But for us priests, how do we really know for certain? When all is said and done, we don't know. But those babies, they're certainly good. There is no doubt about that. That's something you can take to the bank."

Just as it is always a joy for a priest to be able to celebrate a baptism, says Fr. Vaverek, it's always equally edifying to see a married couple who have been coming for counseling turn out the right way. "On a couple of occasions, I've dealt with cases of adultery. The couples reached the point where they understood that this situation did not happen in a vacuum. Even the spouses who had been 'faithful' realized that they had been unfaithful in a variety of other ways that contributed to the bigger problem. To see the kind of reconciliation that can take place is wonderful." Ten years ago, he says, no one would have guessed that some of these couples would still be married a decade later.

But Fr. Vaverek doesn't contend that the priest is ordained to function as a marriage counselor, as a psychologist would. There has been confusion during past decades over the proper role of the priest when it comes to counseling. The priest is not essentially a psychologist; he is a spiritual director. The difference between psychological counseling and spiritual direction is an important one.

Psychological counseling, explains Fr. Vaverek, is geared toward making sure that the psyche is functioning in a healthy and harmonious way, which is very useful in life. "Christ did come to heal us," he points out. More important, perhaps, the spiritual life will have an effect on the life of the psyche. The two are certainly distinct, but the goal of the spiritual life is the flourishing of the human person, body and soul — both of them together.

When Fr. Vaverek counsels a troubled couple, he attempts to guide them in their spiritual life in order to put their problems into proper perspective. In that way, he hopes, a true reconciliation will take place. The same spiritual guidance is given to engaged couples who come to him for marriage preparation. "The tools that we make use of, whether it's some sort of personality inventory, one-on-one discussions with the priest, engaged encounters, or sponsor couples, should all be geared toward getting at what's going on with the couple emotionally, spiritually, and personally," he explains.

With a view toward discovering areas that are going to be particularly troublesome in their relationship, Fr. Vaverek tries to ensure that the couples have a sound grasp of what's going to be required of them in Christian marriage, and that they're going to be in a position, humanly speaking, to be able to make a reasonable and mature decision to undertake this commitment for the rest of their lives. Preparing couples for marriage, witnessing the sacrament of Matrimony, and watching couples grow in their married lives is yet another source of joy in the ministry of priests.

Indeed, for Fr. Vaverek, and for thousands of other priests ordained in the Catholic Church, profound, enduring joy is a remarkable characteristic of this ministry. It is the joy of fatherhood — in Fr. Vaverek's case, a spiritual fatherhood, one that is not unlike natural fatherhood. And that's owing to the very nature of the Catholic priesthood. In fact, it's also the reason Catholic priests are referred to as "Father" throughout Christendom.

In consequence of Catholic belief, administering the sacraments, in addition to preaching the gospel, is of utmost importance to the Catholic priest in any role, especially that of pastor. "Mass is the center point of each day," says Fr. Vaverek. "I say Mass every day. Anyone who is engaged in pastoral ministry — and I've got souls who are under my care — always offers Mass for the souls entrusted to him." And that's what he and other pastors do each and every day, often unbeknown to many lay Catholics.

The celebration of Mass — the source and summit of the Christian life — is a subject dear to Fr. Vaverek. In fact, he has penned several articles on the Liturgy, as well as on church architecture, which, he believes, greatly contributes to the understanding of Catholic worship when properly designed.

"I think, in general, that the current crisis in the Catholic Church owes to the fact that we have not, in an effective manner, taken to heart the gospel and the universal call to holiness based on our full, conscious, and active participation in the Paschal Mystery of Christ, which is focused on a life of prayer, self-denial, and good works," he says.

The problem with many of the abuses of post-Vatican II liturgy, he claims, stems from a fundamental misunderstanding of the Mass and, more specifically, a misunderstanding by priests themselves of their role in Catholic worship. This misunderstanding, says Fr. Vaverek, has too often resulted in an "entertainment model" of liturgy, with the priest acting as a sort of talk-show host. The Mass, however, is the worship of God in union with Christ, which brings glory to God and salvation to the world. The visible, auditory, and other sensory aspects of Catholic worship are designed to draw us into deeper prayerful, contemplative union with Christ.

"These aspects are not intended as entertainment," argues Fr. Vaverek, "nor should they be the things that attract Christians or keep them coming to Mass." A "Mozart Mass" performed by the symphony is entertainment, he says by way of example, but when sung at Mass is prayer — unless the congregation is there for the music rather than for worship. "But it seems to me that the Mass makes for very poor entertainment since its whole structure, movement, and purpose leads to what is invisible, not to the sensible. The beauty and reality of what happens at Mass — the sacramental celebration of Christ's loving Sacrifice — is what is attractive and keeps people coming to Mass. The sensory aspects are meant to draw people more deeply into this sacred mystery. Because entertainment, at least in the West, is not designed to foster contemplation, it is antithetical to the spirit of liturgy." Thus, the priest is not an entertainer.

It is important to realize, notes Fr. Vaverek, that the Church is calling Christians to live the Paschal Mystery, to live the dying and rising of Christ every day, and, when we come to the celebration of the Mass, to allow God to do the work in us by which we are transformed in Christ. Christ makes present for us a gift of Himself to the Father, and His gift of us to the Father. We are invited by the gift of grace to say yes to that and to become part of that offering, to bring that offering of our daily life and our struggles, and to be united deeply to Christ in offering ourselves to God.

"And that needs to be the focus," Fr. Vaverek says.

"If we focus on recognizing Jesus in the people or in the Host or in the Word, we are missing the heart of the matter. After the council, many so-called liturgists said that the people were supposed to focus on the priest, the people, the Host, and the Word. That's all well and good, but it's not the purpose of the Mass. The purpose of the Mass is to make present Christ's saving death and Resurrection: the Sacrifice of the Cross and the banquet of the Lord; it's that first and foremost, and Christ is therefore present in these four other ways. The fundamental key to understanding the Mass, however, is to recognize what's happening here, and that is Christ's gift of Himself, and the gift of us to the Father, and our participation in that."

In many cases, abuses of the Mass have led to a breach of trust in the relationship between the laity and the priests and bishops who serve them. The revelations of widespread sexual abuse by Catholic priests have served to widen that breach to a point that it sometimes seems irreparable.

What we're dealing with here is called "scandal," remarks Fr. Vaverek. Although this may seem obvious to many, understanding just what exactly scandal is — and the nature of scandal, he adds, is very important. The word *scandalize* literally means to place an obstacle in someone's path. Scandal is an attitude or action that fosters the fall of another into sin. "Giving scandal," he explains, is when one is guilty of such an attitude or action. "Taking scandal" is when one falls in response to an offensive attitude or action by another. One avoids taking scandal, Fr. Vaverek often counsels, by not sinning, regardless of what another person does or fails to do, whether that person be a parent, spouse, friend, religious, priest, bishop, or pope. St. Francis de Sales spoke of giving scandal as a form of spiritual murder and taking scandal as a form of spiritual suicide. Christians should avoid both taking or giving scandal, just as they should avoid both murder and suicide.

Fr. Vaverek feels blessed in his ability to deal with scandal in the Church, not because of any wonderful personality trait, but because of what might be described as a forthright Catholic upbringing. His parents, Milton and Sheila, were relatively active in the Church when he was growing up. One would probably consider that they were more active than most young adults at the time.

Spiritual Direction in Scandal-Ridden Times

In 1956, they were drafted by their pastor at St. Michael's Church in Pontiac, Michigan, to teach high school CCD and instruction classes for converts. They were in their early twenties at the time — and that's how they met. They married just a little over a year later.

As various controversies began to unfold after the Second Vatican Council, the Vavereks did not hide from their seven children the fact that grave difficulties were lacerating the life of the Church. "They tried to take the controversies as much in stride as they could," remembers Fr. Vaverek, "and it also helped that we had some exemplary priests in our extended family and others who were very close to us."

He had no illusions regarding the religious and political machinations that take place in the life of the Catholic Church, he adds. In the late Sixties and early Seventies, Fr. Vaverek witnessed or heard of "priests dating openly and marrying; clergy and religious fostering the gravest errors regarding human sexuality; the substitution of New Age gimmicks and pop psychology for Christian spirituality; clergy and bishops ignoring the just concerns of the faithful; and bishops, clergy, and religious lying to each other and the faithful in order to secure political or financial advantages." Given human imperfection and the reality of sinfulness, Fr. Vaverek realized early in life that politics and manipulation are realities that will be present wherever people gather — including in the Church.

"When I thought I might be called to the priesthood," he remembers vividly, "my first thought was, 'Oh, gee, not that mess,' that is, the problems in the Church! I thought, 'Please God, just leave me in peace. I'll raise my family as best I can. I can do that well, but why do I need to get directly involved in this mess by entering the priesthood?' "

Priest

Fr. Vaverek's life unfolded as a Catholic with an awareness of the stark realities of the sometimes all-too-human side of the saints and sinners who make up the Church Militant. To this day, he says, he deals with scandal just as he has dealt with it all his life: "I realize that the Church is Christ's Church, not *our* Church; it cannot be identified with any one group of people — lay, clerical, or religious. We have to realize that there are difficulties in living out our Christian lives, and there are likewise going to be difficulties within the life of the Church, not just with things that are external to the Church, but more often with those things that are internal to the life of the Church. The hope of eradicating such problems is impossible, apart from extraordinary grace in God. It is very important to stick to the duties of state, to realize what is my responsibility and what is not, and to pray for all things, that they will be well, but not to get distracted on crusades that really aren't headed anyplace."

One's state of life, he clarifies, is determined not only by vocation, but by the specifics in which that vocation is lived. A priest's duty of state would therefore vary widely according to his assignment. A common duty is to seek, under God's grace, to live a holy life, to pray for all men, to celebrate the sacraments worthily, especially the Mass, and to guide people into a deeper living of the gospel. Duties that are clearly not the priest's, he says, are to be the bishop or Pope, to be a politician or businessman, and to solve everybody's problems. "To know one's place and keep it" is essential so that a priest may focus on the tasks that are actually his responsibility, rather than getting caught up in situations, large or small, that are not properly his responsibility.

"As fallen human beings, it often proves easier — and more interesting — to get involved in anything *other* than the things assigned by God to our care. This is seen, for example, among priests and parents who are inordinately interested in their careers, financial plans, social activities, et cetera, to the detriment of fostering faith, hope, and love in their parish or family."

Despite being aware of the political machinations in the Church, the Vavereks nevertheless were close friends with many exemplary priests who gave the young Timothy a very positive image of the Catholic priesthood. One family friend, Fr. Charles Pius Wilson, a Dominican priest who had once served as the chaplain at Mrs. Vaverek's boarding school in Michigan, was one of Timothy's role models during his younger days. Even with these positive influences, a vocation to the priesthood was not something he had ever considered while he was growing up. Strong in math and the sciences, Vaverek studied physics while an undergraduate at Southwest Texas State, where he also developed an interest in metaphysics and cosmology.

During his senior year, Vaverek began to discern what he'd study in graduate school. At this point in his life, as well as when he was in high school, he acted on the presumption that he would eventually get married and settle down to have a family, as his father did. It was no surprise, then, that he was concerned with making himself "employable." Continuing in the field of theoretical physics didn't seem to be a practical choice to him because he wasn't interested in becoming a university professor.

The first time the idea that he might have a vocation to the priesthood came to him was when he sat down one day and started to list some of his assets, thinking that this might give him some direction.

The context for his question was, prudently, "What does God want me to do?" rather than what he himself might have wanted to do at that moment. "Now, for whatever reason," he continues, "as I sat down to list what those assets were, the first thing I put down was 'the Faith.' I wouldn't have thought, under most circumstances, that this would be the first thing that would come to mind. But it was. I thought that was kind of odd. And then I started asking the question, 'How can I particularly use the Faith?' And I started getting ugly answers."

He tried to rationalize that he could easily use the Faith well as a husband and father, no matter what career he happened to enter. Yet the priesthood kept coming to mind, and he kept thinking, "No, I don't like that idea!" Over the next couple of weeks, he and God had what he calls "a nice heart-to-heart talk."

"I said, 'Look, I'm nearly twenty years old. I haven't thought of this before in my life. There's no reason at this late date to believe that this is what You want me to do. And I can't be jumping at shadows. This is a time of transition.' My life had always pointed toward marriage and the family — and the sciences. Neither did I think I had a preponderance of evidence to suggest otherwise. I told myself I wasn't going to sweat this, because I didn't really have reason to believe that I was truly called to the priesthood. So I told God, 'If You want me to do something else, You've got to make it happen, because I'm not going to do it on my own. I've been saying my prayers for twenty years now and thinking about what You want me to do, and never before has the priesthood ever come up. I'm on another track, and if You want me to go in some other direction, then it's Your job to make it happen.' "

Vaverek was prepared to enter graduate school at the University of Texas in the Fall of 1980. In fact, that summer he was already registered in summer courses. Then, on July 21 — a Monday he'll never forget — while working through a difficult math problem, he suddenly "became aware" that he was going to be entering the seminary the following month. It wasn't a divine revelation, he says — not something that suddenly imposed itself on his conscience. Rather, it was as if the decision had been made months ago and that it was an established state of mind for him.

"My feeling was, 'Well, I've got just a few weeks before seminary starts.' I didn't hear voices or anything. But then I thought, 'Hey, wait a minute; something's wrong here.' I knew very well that I had not made that decision, so I was kind of in a jam then. On one hand, the idea was there as if it had always been there. On the other hand, I knew full well that it hadn't always been there. There was no doubt then, because I had told God that if He wanted me to do it, He was going to have to make it happen for me. He had just made the decision for me, because I knew that *I* hadn't made the decision."

That day, just a few hours later, he received a letter from the University of Dallas. "I had asked around," he explains, "and found out that it was a good Catholic university. I had been thinking at that time of studying philosophy or theology in graduate school. I had written them to ask about their program."

It had been nearly eight months earlier that he had made the inquiry, and it was in July 21's mail that he received a letter signed by the chairman of the theology department telling him what he'd have to do if he wanted to go to graduate school at the University of Dallas. That same day, Vaverek contacted the vocations director for the Diocese of Austin, and by August 20, he was moving into Holy Trinity Seminary in Dallas and preparing to attend philosophy classes at the University of Dallas as preparation for his future studies in theology.

After a year in Dallas, Vaverek spent his final four years residing at the North American College in Rome, while attending theology courses at the Gregorianum, the Pontifical Gregorian University run by the Jesuits. "It was a great opportunity to be in Rome and to be in Europe," Fr. Vaverek attests, "to be able to be educated with classmates from all over the world, where you have ready access to the living history of the Church. For me, being in Europe was as important or more important than being in Rome. There's the opportunity to travel around Europe and to see those places where the history of my own cultural and religious heritage unfolded."

What Fr. Vaverek means by the "living history" of the Catholic Church is the cultures, the buildings, the art, and the historical places that have been shaped and sustained by the gospel over the centuries. The living history of the Church includes the saints who intercede for us and whose shrines, tombs, and hometowns are sprinkled throughout Europe. The living history of the Church is the one billion souls who today are living the Faith throughout the world and whose compatriots come to Rome to work or study at the various religious institutes, including the Vatican itself. "It's a diverse, chaotic, and messy thing, to be sure," he admits, "but it's a living history guided by the Holy Spirit. And it has given rise to great holiness and beauty along the pilgrim way. All in all, it is a wonder to behold."

Another great advantage of studying in Rome, says Fr. Vaverek, is that the student gets to know the feel of the place that is the epicenter of Catholicism. "It's easy to make Rome either the ideal or some kind of curse," he says. "For many who haven't had the opportunity to come to Rome, the streets are just lined with gold, or the whole place is seen as totally corrupt."

Fr. Vaverek is grateful for the education he received in Rome. He says that if he had studied in the U.S., he likely would have read books written only by American or British authors, or the most popular European theologians whose writings had been translated into English. "We definitely wouldn't have read the classics," he believes.

Spiritual Direction in Scandal-Ridden Times

In Rome, however, he found that his syllabi carried bibliographies from all over the world. At the Gregorianum, the emphasis was on the historical presentation of theology: "We began with the Old Testament and the New Testament, the Patristic period and the Medieval period, and systematically moved our way forward. We didn't always get a uniform treatment of all of those aspects, but the idea was in place that it was important to know the history of the discussion."

In comparison, historical and classical works in the U.S. at that time were largely marginalized. "It wasn't that there were not cutting-edge theologians at the Gregorianum," Fr. Vaverek acknowledges. "Of course there were, and a good part of their classes would be devoted to contemporary thought. The idea was that, in order to study theology, it was important to have these connections across both space and time for your theological formation."

Fr. Vaverek believes that priests, especially diocesan priests, require a broad education because they could be assigned to many different sorts of ministry in the course of their lives. The care of souls requires a deep knowledge of human nature, of the gospel, and of the meaning of the gospel for all aspects of human life. This scholarship is over and above the fundamental need of the priest to know Christ and to live in a deep union with Him according to the virtues and the gifts of the Holy Spirit.

All priests must complete four years of graduate study in theology after having completed college with at least a minor in philosophy. This basic graduate education includes history, philosophy, languages, Scripture studies, canon law, doctrinal theology, liturgy, moral theology, and pastoral practice. Some priests, such as Fr. Vaverek, receive more schooling after ordination as determined by their bishop or religious superior to provide expertise in needed areas of study. These priests might be placed in teaching assignments, in specialized ministries (liturgy, canon law, counseling, spiritual direction, and so on), or they might simply continue in parish ministry, as does Fr. Vaverek.

In 1985, the year Timothy Vaverek was ordained, his older brother Gavin resigned his position at an engineering firm in Longview, Texas, where he had been working for five years, in order to enter seminary. He, too, had discerned that God was calling him to serve the Church as a priest. But Timothy and Gavin weren't the only two of the Vaverek brothers who would be ordained to the priesthood. Their youngest brother, Hayden, who had thought about becoming a priest since he was twelve or thirteen, entered the seminary in 1989. Gavin was ordained in 1990 for the Diocese of Tyler, and Hayden was ordained in 1994 for the Diocese of Charleston, where he serves as a military chaplain for the U.S. Air Force.

Fr. Vaverek is often asked how it is that his one family produced three priestly vocations — something that seems a remarkable achievement in this day. He says the question always reminds him of the story of Fr. Thomas Olmstead, now Bishop of Wichita, Kansas, who was living at the North American College and served as a spiritual director when Vaverek was a seminarian there. "He asked me if any of my brothers were priests," recounts Fr. Vaverek. "I was a little surprised at his question, and he smiled and said, 'Oh no, it's not unusual at all for families to produce more than one priestly vocation.' " In fact, Fr. Vaverek's own diocese, since the 1950s, has had upwards of fourteen or fifteen sets of brothers who were priests. "It was not uncommon," says Fr. Vaverek. "Many of these families produced more than one vocation to the priesthood and sometimes gave daughters to the religious life."

Fr. Vaverek believes this is a reflection on the family life of those who produced multiple vocations. "I've often wondered, and my parents have, too, why the U.S. bishops haven't done a systematic analysis of the families who had more than one vocation to the priesthood or religious life. One would think this would be a worthwhile endeavor."

As for his family, he reports that his home was a truly Catholic one, "but it wasn't like we went to novenas all the time. I think, given the relative strengths and weaknesses of my parents, it was a well-balanced home, psychologically and spiritually. We came to maturity facing the types of problems that everyone experiences, but with basic human and spiritual maturity, so that we could respond to our vocations, whatever those vocations were."

Even now, seventeen years after his ordination, Fr. Vaverek's family plays an important role in his life — and in his priesthood. "I have a good relationship with all my siblings, thanks be to God," he says. "We share the joys and difficulties we are dealing with in our diverse vocations and work environments." The three priests in his family share these ups and downs of priestly life in a particular way and have always supported one another. "The support from my family is vital to me as a priest," he explains, "especially in dealing with the adversities that arise, but also in staying grounded in reality."

Fr. Vaverek acknowledges that it's easy for priests as "authority figures" to become somewhat isolated. As many Catholics know from personal experience, people do not always speak openly and honestly with a priest about his strengths and weaknesses. Fortunately, Fr. Vaverek's large family has never been hesitant in the slightest way to confront him. "It helps, I hope, in preventing me from becoming a 'parody of myself' as I get older. This 'self-parodying' is a rather sad phenomenon that I have seen in priests and other men who enjoy a certain type of authority in the community — doctors, businessmen, lawyers, and so forth."

Fr. Vaverek is reluctant to claim that his family had any kind of "blueprint" for success, beyond saying that his parents lived the Faith, day in and day out. No matter what happened, they always provided a good Christian example of living out the married life. "We were not indoctrinated in any systematic way," he says, "nor were we shielded from the realities of the Church, which remains a source of great blessing — and was especially so in the seminary."

Fr. Vaverek knew that many of his seminary classmates had in fact been shielded from the stark realities in the Church during their formative years. When these students entered the seminary, they tended to be more or less shocked by what was being taught and by what was going on, because they came from places where these perversions of the Faith had not been manifest.

"I distinctly remember," says Fr. Vaverek, "a guy a year ahead of me got very discouraged during his first year away at seminary. His parents sat him down and said, 'Son, this is politics. You can face it in the seminary and in the Church, or you can face it in business or academia. But you don't have a choice about not facing it.' Now, I wouldn't say this guy was naive, but he was shocked nonetheless to find that he had to deal with such things" — politics, political correctness, false teaching, immoral lifestyles, and various other elements of seminary life at that time.

Fr. Vaverek believes the culture wars that have been raging within the walls of the Catholic Church since at least the close of the Second Vatican Council are part of spiritual warfare that always exists — necessarily — in the life of any true believing Christian, regardless of his vocation: "I'd say that life is difficult as a Christian, and it's not safe. Becoming a priest or getting married is not for the fainthearted. You must approach your vocation with open eyes, realizing full well what the nature of the problems are in that particular vocation. If you want a safe path or an easy path, you pretty much have to abandon the Christian life."

For the discerning young man who believes he may be called by God to serve the Church as a Catholic priest, Fr. Vaverek has the same recommendations as he would for anyone who approached him seeking to get his spiritual house in order. He often begins by recommending St. Thérèse's *Story of a Soul* and St. Francis de Sales's *Introduction to the Devout Life*, because both books present a direct and simple spirituality: we grow in the spiritual life by loving God through daily prayer, self-denial, and good works. We live our lives where we are, in the concrete specific circumstances in which we find ourselves each day, and undertake that for the love of God rather than seek some elaborate system of prayer or extraordinary acts of penance.

These classic works, among others, are relevant to Catholics in all ages, Fr. Vaverek says — and always will be. "We know that what these saints did *worked*. We need to start with the basics, and the basics are what we know. When you look across the spectrum of people in such historically, personally, and culturally diverse circumstances as Augustine, Thomas Aquinas, Ignatius, John of the Cross, Teresa of Avila, [John Henry] Newman, and whoever else you want to add to the list, there are certain things that emerge as very clear signposts for the spiritual life. Even though there are differences in time and place, there are still certain things that are universally pertinent: the Christian life entails the Cross, and growth in holiness requires prayer and dedication each day to the state of life that you find yourself in.

"We know that this will lead to times of passive purification of the senses and of the soul. We know these things, and that is not going to change over any amount of time. For someone to be properly aware of the grounding and the basic direction of the spiritual journey, going to the saints and the doctors is not just safe. It's certain; it's true."

Although there are many spiritual parallels between marriage and the priesthood, there is one obvious difference between the two vocations, and this happens to have become one of the most controversial issues in the Catholic Church during the decades following Vatican II: the discipline of celibacy. For Fr. Vaverek, however, the issue was not in the least a controversial one. He never saw celibacy as a deterrent or a stumbling block, either during his seminary years or in his past seventeen years as a priest.

"The issue of whether or not to marry in terms of what I was going to do with my life certainly was an issue," he admits. "But we don't live in abstract worlds; we live where we live under the circumstances in which we find ourselves. Anything else is baloney. The world we live in is with Catholic priests who are celibate. There is no possibility of being a Roman Catholic priest of the Latin rite and being called to marriage. Anything else is a delusion."

The question for Fr. Vaverek was never "Am I called to celibacy?" His vocation revolved not around the issue of celibacy, but around whether he was called to be a priest. "In that context, I certainly had to deal with the reality that I would not be getting married. Yes, it was a sacrifice.

"Something that helped me very much was my understanding of being a father: I could never even envision the possibility of being a priest and being a father. I didn't think that there was any way for me personally to be both. I would not feel I was doing right by either because I can't serve two masters. Those things were clear in my mind." The real issue, he says, comes down simply to how you are emotionally and spiritually going to deal with the fact that you are not going to get married and have a family. "I would say that for me that was always the issue as far as what celibacy calls to mind, never the issue of sex. If God is calling me to the priesthood, then that's where my satisfaction will come from."

Despite Fr. Vaverek's clear understanding of the role of celibacy in the Catholic priesthood, the issue remains seriously misunderstood in modern society, which largely regards celibacy as an unnatural obstacle placed in the path of the cleric by "the medieval Church." What many fail to realize, however, is that Jesus Christ was celibate, even though He, theoretically, could have married. What many more fail to realize is the tradition of "apostolic celibacy"; that is, it was the custom from the beginning of the Church — apostolic times — that priests could be married men *at the time they were ordained*, although no priest was allowed to marry after ordination. In ancient times, these married priests and their wives promised to cease conjugal relations after ordination. This was done, not out of a disregard for sexuality, but "for the sake of the kingdom" (Matt. 19:12) so that the priest could prayerfully dedicate himself to building up the household of the Lord.

And that is how Fr. Timothy Vaverek regards his priestly ministry, as building up the household of the Lord. "It is a task that fills one with great joy. The priesthood is a vocation that is characterized by joy," he says, "but it is also a vocation that demands that you take up the Cross each day and follow Christ. It is a vocation that is neither safe nor easy. The fainthearted need not apply."

That's exactly what Fr. Vaverek continues to do as pastor of St. Joseph's. In his daily life as pastor, he says, his vocation offers him plenty of opportunities to grow in the spiritual life and more than enough opportunities to take up his cross daily. Through prayer, self-denial, and good works, he continues to live "where he is," for better or worse, embedded in the realities of everyday life in Bellmead, Texas.

Chapter 9

Preaching the Gospel, Teaching the Faith

There's a clever old saying: "If you've met one Dominican, you've met one Dominican." Although such a motto seems cheeky to some, since it is a purposeful inversion of a traditional slight against the Jesuits ("If you've met one Jesuit, you've met all Jesuits"), Fr. James Mary Sullivan delights in the saying. In fact, says the Dominican priest, it speaks to the heart of the order's identifying charism.

"Dominican life is a way of being a Christian," he explains, "a way of responding to the good that is placed before him." That individual response, which Christians call *virtue*, is what necessarily differentiates one Dominican from the next. Although there are no cookie-cutter Dominicans, Fr. Sullivan assures us that neither is there the sort of radical autonomy that characterizes some of the more liberal religious orders of the day. To be a Dominican is to live at the heart of the Church.

"One Dominican professor used to tell us that Dominican holiness is a corporate holiness," says Fr. Sullivan, "that we are only as holy as the community in which we live." In fact, it is this "corporate holiness," coupled with the Dominican communal life and choral office, that attracted him to the Order of Preachers.

Priest

When he was a student at Matignon High School in Cambridge, Massachusetts, he took it for granted that he was going to go on to attend the local seminary and be ordained for the Archdiocese of Boston, where he would serve out his ministry as a parish priest. Since the sixth grade, he had never doubted that he would one day serve the Catholic Church through the priesthood. While his high school classmates were applying to schools such as Boston College, Notre Dame, and Georgetown, he applied to Boston's St. John's College Seminary program and was accepted.

But his mother — and God — had other plans for the young Sullivan. "My mom thought I was too young at seventeen to enter seminary, and she urged me to go instead to college," he remembers. "So I thought about that, prayed about it, and talked it over with many people whose opinion I respected." In the end, he says, he concluded that if he truly did have a vocation to the priesthood — as he was certain he did — then it wouldn't just vanish because he attended college. He hadn't considered the possibility that, by attending college, he might become blinded to his vocation and become unable to answer the call, which is a testament to the young man's steadfast desire at the time.

Fortunately, and with God's grace and guidance, Sullivan followed a high school counselor's recommendation to attend Providence College, a relatively small Catholic school in Rhode Island operated by the Dominicans. It was there in Providence that the future Fr. Sullivan would first meet a Dominican priest. In Boston he had never had any contact with the Friars and knew little about them.

Although he was impressed by the Dominican priests he knew on campus, he took little notice of them during his first two years, since he was determined to return to Boston for his seminary studies. During his junior year, however, he took more notice of the

Dominican priory that forms the cornerstone of the college. "What always impressed me," he says of the Providence Dominicans, "was their fidelity to prayer. Each day they would walk across campus in their flowing white habits to attend the community Mass and Office." He couldn't help noticing their presence in the daily life of the college, and he gradually felt drawn more and more to the order.

It was during this third year at Providence College that Sullivan began to explore the possibility that he might have a vocation to a religious order — not necessarily the Dominicans, but the Dominicans on campus had left such an indelible mark on him that he started to feel called to the religious life. Since his uncle was a Redemptorist priest, Sullivan started his exploration with that community, visiting for a vocations weekend. After he had visited a few more religious houses on the East Coast, it became clearer to him that he was being called to serve as a priest, not in a diocese, but in a religious order.

His junior year turned into a year-long search — far and near — for the community to which he was being called. This was his year of discernment. But it wasn't until the beginning of his senior year that he was given his answer. He had narrowed his discernment down to two orders: the Redemptorists and the Dominicans. During an all-night eucharistic-adoration vigil for vocations, he was determined to get that final answer.

"I was there in the chapel all night, praying," he explained, "until about five in the morning, when I finally understood where God was calling me. I was reading through a prayer written by St. Alphonsus Liguori, the founder of the Redemptorists. There was a line in that prayer that says, 'The Lord has called me to this place to thank Him,' and when I prayed that line, it all just became apparent that the Lord was asking me to apply to the Dominicans. I had just finished praying fifteen decades of the Rosary with an elderly Dominican, and I was wiped out. Here was this Redemptorist prayer in a Dominican chapel with a Dominican priest, so I understood then what my next step would be."

Sullivan applied to the Dominicans and was accepted. He entered the Dominican novitiate right after his graduation. "The care that the Dominicans took at Providence College as teachers and preachers was excellent," he says, "but what most attracted me was their common life and the choral office."

Once in the Dominican novitiate at St. Gertrude's Priory in Madeira, Ohio, he would suddenly be fully immersed in that Dominican common life and experience firsthand the daily choral office. "I remember one of the first days of the novitiate, I was standing outside the priory, and I thought to myself, 'Now this is the real thing.' I was done talking about being a priest. I was actually on my way."

The novitiate is a year of intense prayer, when the novice gets immersed in Dominican life, common prayer, private prayer, and study. During classes each week, he studied, among other things, the Dominican Constitutions: the rules and laws of his order. "I thought of it as a spiritual boot camp." One of the most important aspects of the novitiate, he says, is learning how to live a common life, learning how to live with other men.

The second step in the process of Dominican formation is a two-year course in philosophical studies, which he completed in one year, as he already had a degree in philosophy from Providence College. For that year, he lived at the Dominican House of Studies in Washington, D.C., while attending classes at the Catholic University of America.

His philosophy year was followed by five years of theology at the Dominican House of Studies, where he received a Licentiate in

Sacred Theology (S.T.L.). But, as Fr. Sullivan explains, the six years of formation en route to becoming an ordained priest for the Dominicans are much more than years of study and preparation for the priesthood. In addition to taking courses at the House of Studies, there were plenty of obligations to uphold in religious life itself.

"The most important thing was living out the religious vocation, which differs from life as a diocesan priest," he emphasizes. "It's the entire communal life of a Dominican. At the House of Studies, there's common life, there's recreation, common prayer, and private prayer. Part of the beauty for me of the religious life is that it places a balance in one's life. There's a time for prayer; there's a time for community; there's a time for privacy and silence, for study — a time for all those things which can so easily be taken away once you're ordained in the busyness of ordinary life if they're not built up well." The Dominican House of Studies, he says, provided the environment for his study for the priesthood as well as for living a communal religious life.

The Dominicans share much in common with other Catholic religious orders; for example, communal life and common prayer. But the order founded by St. Dominic is unique in many ways. Dominicans, for example, are itinerant. The order is monastic in structure, but not in stability. Being monastic in structure means that the priests and brothers live out their day according to the Liturgy of the Hours. Throughout the day, each Dominican community gathers to sing what they call the choral office, the daily common prayers prescribed by the Church in the Liturgy of the Hours. Praying the Rosary in common and participating in the conventual Mass round out each day. Another important aspect of the monastic structure is dining together at each meal.

But the Dominicans are not monastic in *stability*. That means that each member of the order is moved around wherever he's needed. "St. Dominic's idea of itinerancy," explains Fr. Sullivan, "was a product of his world at the time in which there were very learned monks who, for the most part, remained in their monasteries. If the laypeople didn't visit the monastery, they wouldn't receive the fruits of that learning. On the other hand, the diocesan clergy who staffed the parishes were perhaps zealous and pious men, but too often failed to have the necessary requirements of study."

St. Dominic wanted to combine the best of both worlds, says Fr. Sullivan: the mobility and sacramental presence of the diocesan priesthood and the structure of the monastic life, with its prayer life and rigorous study. "The result is learned preachers," he says. And that's one reason the order is officially called the Order of Preachers (O.P.).

Before founding the new order, St. Dominic was a canon of the Cathedral of Osma in Spain. In other words, he functioned as a diocesan priest who took a vow of "stability" to that particular cathedral. Canons, like Fr. Myron Effing's Canons Regular of Jesus the Lord (see Chapter 3), have an obligation to say the daily Office of the Church in one particular place in order to maintain the Liturgy of the Hours. "That was the life that St. Dominic was living," explains Fr. Sullivan, "when he conceived the idea of a new preaching order."

Dominic was on a diplomatic mission in France with his bishop when they ran across what has become known as the Albigensian heresy (named after the French city of Albi). Albigensians were Catholics who did not know their Faith and had fallen into theological and moral errors. They believed, for example, that the physical world was created by Satan and was evil, and that only the spiritual world, created by God, was good. "One major problem that St. Dominic saw with this false belief," says Fr. Sullivan, "was that it undermined the validity of the sacraments, which are material things. If one believes that all created things are evil, then that undermines even the Incarnation."

In fact, one of the great Dominican saints, Thomas Aquinas, emphasized the Church's true teaching on creation, and, says Fr. Sullivan, there's still an emphasis on this aspect in the study of Aquinas today. "The goodness of creation has always been a hallmark of Dominican thinking and living. The Rosary itself, which is closely identified with the order, begins with the Incarnation, God becoming man, and follows along with all the mysteries which that entails, right up to Mary's Coronation, when she is placed as Queen over all creation, both Heaven and earth."

When Dominic was traveling with his bishop in France, Fr. Sullivan tells the story, he stayed up one night to talk with an innkeeper who was an Albigensian. By morning, Dominic had converted the man. "He won him over by the sacrifices he made," he says, "and St. Dominic knew then that he couldn't return to Osma. He was called to preach among the people who needed to be taught the true Faith."

St. Dominic understood that the proper response to these heretics was to preach to them the true Faith. Once it is preached to them, he knew, they would naturally be attracted to its beauty and desire it. "St. Dominic committed himself to that, and for ten years, from 1206 to 1216, he lived the life of an itinerant preacher," explains Fr. Sullivan, "going to inns, which were the equivalent of modern-day bars, town centers, anywhere he was needed. He even held public debates with the heretics, and there were many miracles and conversions associated with that."

In the thirteenth century, the title of "preacher" was reserved to bishops alone. It was not the regular function of the parish priest to preach. St. Dominic's new order was the first "preaching order," and that carried with it a serious charge and privilege. Thus, Dominic combined the study and prayer life of a monk with the itinerancy of a traveling preacher in order to convert souls.

"We wear a habit as a monk would," explains Fr. Sullivan. "We lead a communal life as a monk would, yet we are mobile. We are not bound to one particular priory. We move from priory to priory, depending on where we're needed. It's the same idea today that St. Dominic had eight hundred years ago."

Not only is the Dominican mission the same as it was eight hundred years ago, but the Dominican habit remains much the same as its medieval forbear. Although some people today think such "costumes" are mere silliness and, further, impractical, Fr. Sullivan defends the habit as having enduring significance and deep meaning. He explains it as a "gift from God."

"It's always good to avoid thinking that we in the twenty-first century know so much more than those in the thirteenth century. That's temporal superiority, and a lot of people today suffer from that," he says. The habit makes as much sense today, he insists, as it did in the time of St. Dominic: "For us the habit is something that we receive. We are vested in it. When we begin our novitiate, we don't just go into another room and change into our new habit; we kneel before the Provincial, and he dresses us in it. In that way, it is a powerful reminder of what any religious would be called to — and what a Dominican is called to — a specific Christian way of life that the Lord is giving us. We are receiving a gift from Him. We receive this new habit in order to begin our new way of life."

The habit also serves as a constant reminder of all three religious vows that are taken by the Dominicans, Fr. Sullivan says: "Poverty, because we don't own or wear our own clothes; we wear the habit of the community. Chastity, because we are covered in

modesty. And obedience, because the habit reminds us that we belong to a community, that we are bound together in obedience to
live a certain type of life."

These three vows play a significant role in the life of any religious priest, but especially for the Dominican, says Fr. Sullivan. At
the end of his novitiate year, he made what is known as a "simple
profession." This entailed taking the vows of poverty, chastity, and
obedience for a period of three and a half years. Then Fr. Sullivan,
following Dominican tradition, made his "solemn profession,"
which follows the same formula, except this time he took his vows
"until death."

"There's a beautiful passage, in the First Letter of St. John,[4]
that explains that, due to Original Sin, there's something that the
Catechism calls 'triple concupiscence' [*Catechism of the Catholic
Church*, par. 377]. First, it is subjection to the pleasures of this
world; second, a covetousness of the goods of this world; and finally self-assertion contrary to reason.

"Those three aspects are what the religious vows set out to set
aright. Chastity sets aright subjugation to the pleasures of this
world, because chastity also embraces temperance and fortitude.
This is a Dominican approach to the vows, I would say, and a Dominican way of understanding Original Sin, that the damage ef-
fected by Original Sin doesn't require throwing everything out. If
you pick up a delicate mechanical clock and shake it violently, it's
not going to fare very well, but if you put it back on the mantel-
piece, all the pieces of the clock are still there; they're just out of
order with each other. What they need is the careful hand of an

---

[4] "For all that is in the world, the lust of the flesh and the lust of the
eyes and the pride of life, is not of the Father but of the world" (1
John 2:16).

artisan to put them back together properly and set the clock back into proper working order. You don't throw away the clock; you put the inner workings back into place."

The vows of religious life, says Fr. Sullivan, have helped him live a life of proper order: "The one thing that a Dominican does, and this goes back to the founding of the order, is that when we make religious profession, we only profess obedience, we only say the word *obedience*. We don't mention poverty or chastity in our profession formula. We live by them, of course, because that's how the vow of obedience is understood. We promise obedience to God, the Blessed Mother, St. Dominic, our superiors, and the Constitutions of the order, which require poverty and chastity. In a spiritual way, it's probably the most difficult to give up one's own will, and that may be why obedience is emphasized first and foremost in the life of a Dominican."

Fr. Sullivan doesn't look on his vows as repressive limitations — in fact, quite the contrary. The three vows assist the priest in leading a happy life, just as any Christian vocation properly lived is a healthy way of life. "Following the vows," he explains, "is a healthy way of life because they address the basic human needs we all have. Those include the pleasures of this world, the goods of this world, and self-will. Each one of the three contains something that is good. Chastity, for example, doesn't mean that pleasure is evil, but it does mean that I have sacrificed sexual pleasure for the sake of Christ. It means that I am not ruled by my passions. The same is true with obedience. Just this summer, my Provincial asked me to act as Provincial Promoter for the Third Order of St. Dominic, the Lay Dominican Community in New York City. It was in an act of obedience that I happily undertook that task. The vow is made more a reality when I am actively obeying my superior."

Another distinguishing quality of the Dominican Order is that it's primarily clerical. The friars are meant to serve the Church as priests, although a very few members of the order are brothers. "The sacramental presence of Christ was not detached from His preaching," explains Fr. Sullivan, "because preaching can bear its fruits only in receiving the grace of the sacraments, whether you move someone to conversion and have him come to Confession, or whether you teach someone about the reality of the Holy Eucharist, and he receives it with a more open embrace."

In the thirteenth-century world of St. Dominic, the centers of learning were to be found at places such as Paris, Oxford, and Bologna. These university centers are where the Dominicans went to preach. "That's where they were needed at that time," says Fr. Sullivan, "so that's where they went. The Dominicans founded priories in these places, such as Blackfriars College at Oxford University and Saint Jacques in Paris, and began to attract vocations there."

Over the centuries, the Dominicans have built a reputation of being one of the more intellectual orders, and that is still true today. "Our student brothers right now are very academically oriented and gifted," says Fr. Sullivan. "Some have already earned Master's or doctoral degrees before they joined the Dominicans, so that's a great resource for the order."

Probably the greatest distinguishing quality of the Dominicans is the charism of preaching. "Dominican identity finds its greatest expression in preaching," Fr. Sullivan explains, "and in the proclamation of the gospel. Every other aspect of Dominican life — the vows of obedience, chastity, and poverty, the common prayer of the Liturgy of the Hours, study, and communal life — are all meant to form and nourish a preacher who proclaims the gospel out of his own contemplative prayer."

Consequently, Fr. Sullivan defines his priestly ministry as a preacher. Since he was ordained in 1995, he has served as an associate pastor, a retreat master, and a seminary professor, but in each of these positions, he says, he has always understood himself primarily as a preacher of the gospel. He may do it in a new way and to a different audience, depending on his assignment, but to Fr. Sullivan, it is all a way of preaching the gospel.

His present "preaching assignment" is Professor of Dogmatic Theology at St. Joseph's Seminary-Dunwoodie in the Archdiocese of New York, where he teaches courses on the sacraments, Christology, and Christian Anthropology as well as a *Catechism* course. "It's an awesome privilege to teach here," he says, "because I am involved in the formation of future priests." In short, his present assignment as an itinerant preacher is to preach the gospel to seminarians who are being formed to be configured to Christ in the sacrament of Holy Orders. "The word *seminary* denotes a certain type of greenhouse," he explains, "that is, taking care of growing plants or seedlings. No one who comes here is ready to be ordained, and no one who leaves here is worthy to be ordained. And so it's a matter of helping these men, first and foremost by the example of my own life, and by handing on what I've learned from my own priesthood.

"One of the ways in which I try to do this is by teaching them what is practical for them. I remember learning lots of things in my seminary days that I don't think I ever used again. I try to teach some things that are helpful for them in answering questions that people will come to them with. For example, last semester, we had Christian Anthropology, and during the first half of the course, I used the *Summa Theologiae* of St. Thomas Aquinas to cover creation, Providence, the angels, Original Sin, et cetera. In the second half of the course, I used the Holy Father's *Theology of the Body* and went through those papal addresses, because I think there's a great wealth there. Future priests need to know how that will impact the parishes in which they will work. I don't think that a seminary is a graduate school of theology. In some ways, it is not academic. It's formative. We're not teaching them to pass a test. We're teaching them to live a life."

Before moving to St. Joseph's Seminary, he was assigned to St. Stephen's Priory in Dover, Massachusetts, where he preached retreats and traveled around the country, giving parish missions. Whether it was in Boston, Chicago, Los Angeles, or Columbus, Ohio, people expressed the same desire: to hear the Catholic Faith preached in all its fullness, both the beauty and the burden.

For four years before that, Fr. Sullivan cut his teeth as a newly ordained Dominican priest at St. Gertrude's Priory and Parish in Madeira, Ohio, the same place he completed his novitiate formation. Aside from the primary tasks of celebrating the sacraments, his "preaching assignment" at the parish was catechetically oriented: education. "I think it's very Dominican to be involved in what we would now call adult education or faith formation. As St. Paul says in Romans 10:14: 'And how are they to believe in Him of whom they have never heard? And how are they to hear without a preacher?'"

Fr. Sullivan served the parish in the four years leading up to the Great Jubilee of the year 2000, which provided an extra incentive and initiative for Catholics to become more knowledgeable about their Faith. Since the *Catechism* had been published just a few years before he arrived there, he used that tremendous resource, which he calls "the greatest gift of the Holy Father's pontificate," to teach the Faith. First, he began publishing a weekly column in the parish bulletin, each week discussing a different section of the *Catechism*, something that parishioners found very helpful.

Fr. Sullivan also started a weekly lecture series that quickly became very popular. "I called them the Millennium Lectures, because they were geared toward preparing parishioners for the new millennium." Each week a different topic was addressed through the use of Scripture, the *Catechism*, and papal encyclicals. Each week the lectures attracted between seventy-five and a hundred people, some of whom traveled from distant parishes to hear Fr. Sullivan preach.

He particularly liked to work with young adults, whom he found very interested in learning more about their Faith, since many of them who had come of age in the 1970s and 1980s were educated without the benefit of the *Catechism* and were often confused about what the Church teaches and how to live according to God's will. To address that need, Fr. Sullivan started a group called "Generation Christ" — a takeoff on "Generation X." During their weekly Sunday-evening meetings, the group discussed Catholic books, listened to guest speakers, and participated in open question-and-answer forums. Each of the meetings ended with Compline, the night prayer of the Liturgy of the Hours.

Generation Christ provided not only a great place for young adult Catholics (in their thirties and forties) to learn more about their Faith, but also the kind of social atmosphere where they could meet others their age who shared the same values and love for God and the Catholic Church. "I would say that one of the things that made it most successful," says Fr. Sullivan, "is that it was not primarily a social group. We were all there because we wanted to learn more about our Faith. There were social aspects, of course, but that wasn't the point of coming together; we were there to learn about Christ." Nonetheless, Generation Christ has already led to at least three marriages between regular participants, and the group continues to meet on Sunday nights, even after Fr. Sullivan left them in 2000. It has now spread to Washington, D.C.; Steubenville, Ohio; and Pleasantville, New York.

In all these different "preaching assignments," Fr. Sullivan has always believed that he's living out his religious life as any Dominican is meant to. "It's a happy life," he reiterates again and again, and anyone who knows Fr. James Sullivan knows him as the happy priest that he is. Above all, he says, "to be a Dominican means for me to respond to the Lord's call to save my soul and to help others be saved. That's why we exist." Accordingly, Fr. Sullivan is known as a faithful man of prayer, a man of study, and a man of service, and, he says, he will continue with God's grace to be such a priest "until death."

Chapter 10

Working for Small Rewards —
One Human Life at a Time

Rosary in hand, Fr. Paul Berschied leads hundreds of Catholics down to an Ohio Planned Parenthood clinic, which takes the lives of three thousand unborn babies each year. The group he leads, Helpers of God's Precious Infants, seeks an end to abortion through prayer. "There's no talking, no sign carrying," Fr. Berschied explains. "The only thing we do is pray the Rosary — all fifteen decades. Our intention is the conversion of hearts that will ultimately lead to an end to abortion."

Fr. Berschied and two other priests have been doing this once a month for six years now. Each march begins with a "Pro-Life Mass" followed by eucharistic adoration and a Rosary procession from the church to the local abortion center — a distance of three blocks. Some remain in the church to pray in front of the Blessed Sacrament, but most join the peaceful march to the clinic.

Several other priests have joined Fr. Berschied over the years in this growing apostolate, and it is quite a sight to see four hundred Catholics standing shoulder-to-shoulder on the sidewalk in front of Planned Parenthood. Those who have witnessed the march, including mothers approaching the clinic both by car and on foot, have been deeply impressed by the peaceful gathering. It has also left an indelible mark on many of those who have themselves participated in the Rosary procession.

In 1997, Fr. Berschied and the others participating in the inaugural procession arrived at the abortion clinic to find uniformed "clinic escorts" at the entrance. "It was good to see some of these clinic workers in the flesh," says Fr. Berschied. "That way we knew who we were praying for." That's an important part of this priest's pro-life mission. "We're not trying to change the institution. We're trying to convert individuals — live people with flesh like ours and blood coursing through their veins."

He's adamant about his focus on individual conversion, he says, because "we cannot change institutions. Jesus never even gave the first thought to changing institutions. There was great pressure by His own people, the Zealots, to change the institutions of the Roman Empire. He wouldn't. Instead, He changed people one person at a time. He converted the Roman centurion who asked for the cure of his son. He changed the Roman soldier who asked for the cure of his servant. He changed the hearts of individuals one at a time, thus bringing about the sanctification of the world."

All Christians, Fr. Berschied says, must understand this and do likewise. The part the priest must undertake in this mission is to confect the Eucharist, to bring the sacraments to the people, and to sanctify them so that they can carry on the work of discipleship, which means going into the world, sharing the Faith, and living worthy Christian lives that will serve as examples for others.

He doesn't know whether any of the clinic workers have been converted directly because of his work with the Helpers of God's Precious Infants. In fact, he realizes that he may never see with his own eyes the good fruits of his labors in this ministry and others.

Nevertheless, he says, "we have to keep persevering, just as the People of God waited thousands of years for the Savior to come, and just as we have been waiting a long time for His second coming. We must continue to do His work by converting individuals."

Sometimes, however, God grants the gift of seeing the fruits of these intense labors. Fr. Berschied knows that the Helpers group has indeed changed some individuals and even saved some children from imminent slaughter. "In the past six years, I know that we've saved at least six babies, and I can only imagine that we've saved many more," he says. "Some mothers have told us on the spot, right in front of the clinic while we're praying that they've changed their minds, and they accepted transportation to a pro-life pregnancy center instead of going ahead with their scheduled abortion." On several other occasions Fr. Berschied was called and told by women that the presence of the Helpers group dissuaded them from obtaining abortions. They said they came to the clinic, witnessed the peaceful Rosary procession, and turned around and went straight back home. Other mothers who did have abortions later came to him for counseling. "Being a part of this movement has allowed me to reach out to women predominantly, but more recently also men who are 'post-abortive,' " Fr. Berschied says. "Popular myths to the contrary, post-abortion syndrome exists for both men and women, and it is not nice."

Another positive fruit from the Helpers apostolate, he adds, is that it seems to have spawned a tremendous increase in pro-life activities in Fr. Berschied's home diocese of Covington, Kentucky. "We bring people in from many different parishes. It's a very strong lay-driven movement under the direction of a priest." He believes this effort is exemplary in showing the kind of balance between priests and the laity that Christ desires for His Church: "This good work wouldn't happen without the help of dedicated laypeople."

Priest

Some today are fond of reminding Catholics that a priest isn't needed to lead prayers, that a priest isn't needed to lead pro-life activities, and that in fact, if you look at some of the most successful pro-life organizations in the country, you'll find that they're led not by priests, but by laypeople. This argument, however, dismisses both the efficacy of ministerial leadership and the spiritual good of combining the sacraments with pro-life efforts. The question goes to the heart of the priesthood and its intimate connection to the sacraments. Fr. Berschied explains: "The purpose for the priest is to sanctify the people who will, in turn, sanctify the world. Priests sanctify their people by preaching the gospel, celebrating the Eucharist, and administering the sacraments to the people for their benefit and to give greater honor and glory to God."

Not all of Fr. Berschied's pro-life work is specifically geared toward an end to abortion. Even with Helpers of God's Precious Infants, there are other important pro-life benefits that many overlook. In this case, for example, a collection of hundreds of dollars is taken up during the Helpers' Mass each month, with half used for the ministry and the other half donated to a poor inner-city parish that does a lot of charity work in its neighborhood. With that money, the church has been able to help pay the rent of parishioners in a tight spot and to help to put food on the table of families whose fathers or mothers have lost their jobs. "It's a wonderful thing, because we go there to peacefully pray for an end to abortion," he says, "and at the same time we are taking care of the poor. So we put our money where our mouth is, which is exactly what abortion proponents often accuse pro-life groups of not doing." Of course, it's the Catholic Church, with her stalwart pro-life teachings — not places like Planned Parenthood — that runs adoption agencies, hospitals, schools, soup kitchens, and crisis pregnancy centers.

Another pressing moral concern of the day is that of euthanasia, ending the life of a human person against the will of God. Fr. Berschied's pro-life response to that is to assist the indigent who are terminally ill. For the past several years, he has served as a spiritual director to the Mary Rose Mission, a Catholic-run hospice in Covington, Kentucky. In that capacity, he attends board meetings, visits patients, and gives advice and spiritual direction to the overall operation.

The Mission, he says, is yet another excellent example of a lay-run apostolate assisted in the spiritual realm by a priest. "Over ninety percent of the patients at the Mary Rose Mission either seek Baptism, convert to the Catholic Church, or return to Catholicism before dying." The important factor, he believes, is that the "unadulterated truth" is presented in a caring and compassionate manner by orthodox Catholics. For that, God seems to be blessing their work abundantly. "It is very much a pro-life mission," he says. "The Mission is helping people at the end of their lives when so many people just want to euthanize them."

The operating principle in this work is also converting the hearts of individuals and bringing them to Christ. Although Fr. Berschied regards conversions as rewards in the life of a priest, he sees the intrinsic worth in doing God's will and serving the Church with an undivided heart. This intrinsic worth is of no little importance, because in today's priesthood, one of the difficulties is that priests, like everyone else — doctors, lawyers, teachers, architects — want to be rewarded for the work they've done. They would naturally like to have specific physical evidence of what they've achieved through their labors. The doctor holds the babies he delivers; the architect sees the building he has designed; the author reads the book he has written. More often than not, however, the priest can't visibly see the good fruits of his work.

"That's why the intrinsic worth of the priesthood has got to be in doing God's will," says Fr. Berschied. "God's will might be for us to sit in a cave and pray, and we may never see anyone benefit from that, but the intrinsic worth, nonetheless, is in knowing that we're doing what God has asked us to do."

Nevertheless, Fr. Berschied, like everyone else, is delighted whenever he can witness the fruits of his work, as in the case of the women who turn away from abortion, or the terminally ill who embrace God before death. But even much less drastic "evidence" is a delight, he admits. "Sometimes you see married couples living their Faith by adhering to *Humanae Vitae* or embracing the fullness of what John Paul II called the 'splendor of truth.'"

He remembers a couple who came to him a few years ago for marriage preparation. They considered themselves Catholic, he explains, although they had already been living together for several years and had a child. "I told them that if they wanted to be Catholic, they needed to start living a Catholic life," he explains, "and that meant proper preparation for marriage."

Normally, he doesn't agree to marry couples who are already living together as man and wife. He requires them to move apart and live celibate lives for the six-month preparation period. In the case of a couple with a child, he requires them to live celibate lives and sleep in separate bedrooms for the duration of that six-month period.

"This particular couple did," he says, "and their lives changed. As a result of the marriage preparation, which involved learning about the teachings of the Church, they embraced *Humanae Vitae* by stopping their use of contraceptives. They now have several more children, and are very involved at the parish, especially in pro-life activities. They have visibly grown in their love of the Church, and they appear to be leading exemplary Christian lives precisely because they have accepted and practice the teachings of the Catholic Church."

Fr. Berschied has seen other couples in his parish embrace Natural Family Planning and *Humanae Vitae*. Their lives visibly changed, too, he says. "They had more children, and they led happier family lives." Fr. Berschied has also witnessed some parishioners come back to the practice of the Faith after being away for as many as thirty or forty years.

One particular family conversion comes to his mind. He once had a student who attended St. Cecilia's School who had never been baptized; his parents were Catholics, although very much inactive in the Faith. "He was really going in the wrong direction," Fr. Berschied remembers. "But when he learned about the sacrament of Baptism, what it really was, during his religion class, he developed a strong desire for it." Later that year, Fr. Berschied baptized the young man and gave him his First Communion. "As a result, his entire family came back to the Church, and the boy is now a different kid." A few years later, the student wrote a school essay about how the Church had completely changed his life. "Whereas before, he was withdrawn and wouldn't talk at times," remarks Fr. Berschied, "his reception of the sacraments changed him."

In addition to his work as pastor and his innumerable pro-life efforts, Fr. Berschied volunteers as a chaplain to the local police department, in which capacity he has also witnessed his share of conversions and changed lives. The purpose of the police chaplain program, he explains, is primarily to assist the patrol officers. He rides along with them at times to get to know them. During these ride-alongs, Fr. Berschied is sometimes called on by the officers to assist in domestic-dispute calls as a part of the police's quick-intervention plan. In other instances, he has been asked to talk with criminals and aid in guiding them to long-term assistance.

One evening, he says, he was riding in a patrol car with an officer when they received a call that led to the arrest of several teenagers caught in the act of malicious mischief. They had been shooting paint balls at cars, street signs, stores, and even a horse. Fr. Berschied recognized one of the teens as a former parishioner who had left his parish after his freshman year in high school. He was now eighteen years old, which meant that, if arrested, he would receive much harsher penalties than the others who were arrested as juveniles, plus a permanent record.

"Because I was on duty that night and called to the scene," Fr. Berschied explains, "I spoke to the eighteen-year-old and told him to contact me the next day, which he did." Later the priest met with the captain, the sergeant, and the patrol officer to request a "diversion program" for the young man. Fr. Berschied's plan was approved by the police and by the young man's parents, who were grateful for the assistance he was offering.

The teen was sentenced to perform forty hours of community service under Fr. Berschied's direction and supervision and was to be monitored for a year, much as if he had been placed on probation. His grades, his activities — everything — had to be reported to the police chaplain. According to Fr. Berschied, all went well, and the teen not only completed his required hours, but performed an additional twenty hours of community service on his own. His criminal offense was expunged from his permanent record.

"It took a lot of time," reports Fr. Berschied, "but perhaps we saved a kid from doing something worse in the future, or at the very least from having a police record. The police department was very cooperative, and the parents were pleased at the outcome, including the fact that the young man returned to church."

As a police chaplain, Fr. Berschied has also found himself called upon to be the bearer of bad news, delivering death notices.

Working for Small Rewards

When someone dies in a car accident or commits suicide, for example, he assists the officer in delivering the news to family members, always in person. "There's a lot of grief counseling involved in being a police chaplain," he explains. Principally, however, the police chaplain helps the officers confront the traumatic events — deaths, serious accidents, suicides, murders, child-abuse problems, and SIDS (sudden infant death syndrome) — that they encounter in the course of their work. "Trauma is very hard on anyone," he says, "and that includes police officers, who see more than their share by the very nature of their work. The criminal element they experience on a regular basis is especially difficult." Locally, he says, the chaplain program is seen as a highly effective deterrent to officer stress and suicide.

Consequently, Fr. Berschied does a lot of listening and plenty of counseling along the way. Again, he feels that the intrinsic worth of this work is in knowing that he's doing the will of God. After all, he doesn't receive a paycheck for being a police chaplain or a pro-life missionary — not a dime. Such activities would be considered by most working Americans above and beyond the call of duty. But, says Fr. Berschied, the life of a priest is different. Nothing is exactly above and beyond the call of duty when a priest is simply following God's will in his life.

In his work as police chaplain over the past several years, just as with his pro-life activities, Fr. Berschied has been granted the grace of seeing the good fruits of his labors. He has made a few converts on the police force — all of them previously baptized Christians of another denomination. Four others came back to the practice of the Catholic Faith through the presence and influence of the priest. Fr. Berschied and another officer now direct a weekly bible study and prayer group for police officers from all departments.

The officers who converted did so for a variety of reasons, many of those the same reasons anyone might convert to the Catholic Faith. "Police officers tend to be far more spiritual than the average person would think," Fr. Berschied observes. "They are in general well trained, well educated, intelligent men and women. They have questions about religion and about the Catholic Faith, and they aren't shy about asking them. On the whole, they seem inherently to desire to know the truth."

The officers he has converted have been attracted to the beauty of Catholic worship, and more in particular to the Church's teachings regarding family life and societal values. The hierarchical nature of the Church and the historical basis of Catholicism throughout human history and its roots in Judaism have also been appealing to some, he says. "Even then, though, other officers have said to me in a half-serious, half-joking manner that Catholicism would be the last religion they would join, even though they have an enormous respect for the uncompromising teachings of the Catholic Church, especially in pro-life matters."

Not surprising, perhaps, several of the officers have also remarked that they're impressed that Fr. Berschied wears his "uniform" — black clerics and Roman collar — all the time. They get the impression that he's always "on duty" — an impression that is, of course, correct. The officers, he says, are attracted to a Faith that could move a man to dedicate not just his job to serving others, but his entire *life*, on a 24-7-365 basis.

"The vocation to the priesthood," explains Fr. Berschied, "requires single-minded dedication and service to God and to His Church, to the elimination of all else." That, he says, is the primary reason why, in the Latin rite, priests take a vow of celibacy and don't marry. He doesn't look at celibacy as a "necessary evil," but rather as a positive attribute, a "gift" given to him by God to assist him in his vocation to the priesthood. "Personally," he says, "I would find it very difficult, if not impossible, to have a wife and children while giving myself fully to the people of my parish. It would cause a division that I do not believe could be easily sustained, if at all."

Unlike the lay vocation, the priest is expected to direct himself as much as possible to the spiritual dimension and the religious world. "As a priest," he explains, "you have got to spend a particular time in prayer every day. You have to remain recollected every day, and that is difficult if you're doing another job. Almost all priestly positions, such as pastoring, teaching, or a chaplaincy, lend themselves to operating very close to that spiritual realm." In contrast, he says, it would be very difficult to maintain one's priesthood while working in a factory.

There's much to learn, Fr. Berschied believes, from the priests in Russia under Communist rule who were forced into secular labor after losing their churches and all of their possessions. "They fought so hard to maintain their priesthood despite all the horrors and hardships that were forced upon them in the secular domain," he says. These priests were in and out of prisons and gulags; they were constantly under surveillance, and often harassed by guards and the secret police. "My understanding," says Fr. Berschied, "is that these priests were men of deep prayer who rose to the challenge of a sort of martyrdom by offering their lives up for the people."

Just as the Russian priests did last century, so Fr. Berschied focuses his daily life on following the will of the Father by living the life of Christ and keeping Him uppermost in his mind throughout every single day of the year. Yet this is much more than simply a quaint ideal, as it may seem to some today. Following the will of Christ in everyday life is not without its many crosses.

Priest

"The vocation to the priesthood itself is not a cross," he clarifies, "but as any priest will tell you, many crosses present themselves to priests, and the only authentic response is to embrace them as Jesus embraced the Holy Cross." Fr. Berschied recalls emerging from Union Station in Washington, D.C., one year to attend a pro-life demonstration on the Mall. Before he could even set foot off the curb in the nation's capital, he was confronted by an angry man who rushed the priest as if he were going to strike him. "I don't know if it was my Roman collar or my pro-life pin that set him off," he recalls. Fortunately the man "stopped short of an attack and just spit in my face."

Many of these crosses, however, are not necessarily specific to the priesthood, although their degree may be different, depending on the situation. "I have to bear many of the same crosses my father bore," says Fr. Berschied. Such a realization is a testament to the fatherhood aspect of the priesthood. "As a priest, you have to provide for all the needs of the people you are ordained to serve. There are worries and there is loneliness in the priesthood, just as there is in married life. I think one of the great misunderstandings of the modern world is that priests are somehow different from other people on a basic human level. They are not. We have the same expectations and experience the same joys, the same hurts, and the same tragedies. They are just manifested in a different way and to a different degree."

He still recalls many difficult days his family experienced when he was a child: "I can only imagine what it was like for my parents when money was tight, and it was difficult to have food on the table at dinner each night. I can't remember the last time I've missed a meal as a priest. There's always been a roof over my head and food on my table, and in that way, there are many worries a priest doesn't have that a married couple might be burdened with over a whole lifetime. For priests, perhaps that's compensation for being available for our people twenty-four hours a day."

Other crosses, he admits, are a bit more unique to the priesthood. The massive scandal of clergy sexual abuse is one such cross. The evil actions of certain priests and the accompanying tabloid bonanza is, without a doubt, a major wound to the priesthood. The scandal has caused many people, Catholics and non-Catholics, to re-evaluate the way they think about the priesthood and the way they treat priests.

"All of us in the Church — bishops, priests, religious, and laity — are injured when someone in the Church fails in discipleship," says Fr. Berschied, especially when that failure involves a heinous evil and perhaps one of the most despised crimes in the history of the world. It's easy for many Catholics to lose hope in the Church, he acknowledges, but at the same time, his first operating principle in dealing with scandal — even scandal of such proportion — is to realize that our love for the Church and our faith, hope, and trust in the Church are totally dependent upon Jesus Christ.

"If we love Jesus, we will love the Church," he says. Yet in the same breath, he admits that Catholics are not to accept just any teaching or action coming from a priest or bishop. Their teachings and their actions both must be in line with the teachings of the Church's Magisterium. Otherwise, all they are doing is being unfaithful and abusing their trusted positions of authority. "This is all part of the Cross," he says. "The suffering is there, and we have to embrace it by remaining strong and true in our Faith. Only in that way will we overcome such obstacles and difficulties."

Thus, he says, embracing the Cross is the first step to becoming a "good priest," something he feels all priests strive for. So, what makes a good priest? Fr. Berschied says a good priest is "a man who is truly in love with Christ and His Church, who desires and develops a very strong personal relationship with Jesus, loves the Holy Mass, and lives a prayerful and Eucharistic life, which includes praying the Divine Office [Liturgy of the Hours] every day, being recollected throughout the day, and making visits to the Blessed Sacrament whenever he can. And devotion to the Blessed Mother sustains the priest as he attempts to do the work of her Son, Jesus."

In short, it is prayer and the sacraments — the Holy Eucharist, the Divine Office, and the Rosary — that ground the priest in his everyday life. The Catholic Church teaches, Fr. Berschied emphasizes, that the priest acts *in persona Christi* and as an *alter Christus* ("another Christ"), and thus the priest must enter into the life of Christ as profoundly as possible. "It is through the re-presentation of our Lord's Sacrifice on Calvary that the priest does this best," he explains.

Although the priest, by virtue of his ordination, serves as a vehicle through whom Christ works, he is no longer who he was before ordination, but truly changed to be as like unto Christ as possible, so that the specific mission of Christ can be continued in the world today. Priests, he says, are called to be set apart by God and His Church for the specific act of self-sacrifice for the people of God: "No longer does the priest live for himself, but rather for Christ and for others."

It is for this reason, Fr. Berschied stresses, that the pledge of obedience to the Catholic Church and her teachings is so terribly important in the life of a priest. "A priest must remain united with the Church regarding her morals and her doctrines," he explains. "A failure in this area is what can begin to lead a priest into a loss of personal identity in terms of who he is and what he is to do. This, then, begins the rather vicious cycle of a priest turning within himself and oftentimes developing personal problems that are more often today referred to as 'inappropriate behaviors.' The life of a priest must be a constant turning outwards, as was the life of Christ in His public ministry. Even when Christ went to pray in private, He was in essence turning out and looking toward the Father. Christ did not go into Himself to find Himself, but rather to His Father, with whom He is one."

It was this sense of fidelity to the Church by the priests he came to know as a boy in Paducah, Kentucky, that attracted Fr. Berschied to the ministry of the priesthood. His earliest recollection dates from grammar school. "I remember being inspired by the Passionist Fathers who preached a Lenten mission at my parish each year," he recalls. They were his first inspiration to the vocation.

The two pastors he had as a child, Fr. DiNardi and Msgr. Thompson before that, also played no little role in fostering his budding vocation. "They were very faithful," Fr. Berschied remembers above all else. "I would say they were strong men of truth, and they were very prayerful."

What inspired him most during childhood, he says, was serving Mass for them: "I thought there wasn't anything better than to serve at Mass. I started as soon as I could learn all the Latin responses, and you had to know them all. I always felt so comfortable serving Mass." He still believes that serving is one of the best ways to encourage boys to consider the priesthood.

During eighth grade, Fr. Berschied expressed an interest in attending a high school seminary for the Passionists. His bishop, however, derailed that desire, telling him that if he was interested in the priesthood, he would attend a diocesan seminary school at St. Thomas in Louisville. Although he studied there for four years, sponsored by the Diocese of Owensboro, after his high school graduation, the young Berschied went in another direction — at least for a while. Instead of continuing on in seminary, he attended a small liberal-arts college. Since his interests were broad, he emerged from college with aspirations to teach. Not only did he teach; he later became a principal for an inner-city school in Lexington.

After thirteen years in the teaching profession, he found himself again thinking about the priesthood. It wasn't until he attended an ordination ceremony that he realized that was what he was supposed to do. He was thirty-three at the time he resumed his seminary studies at the Pontifical College Josephinum in Columbus, Ohio.

It was no little sacrifice to part with his way of life for the unknown of a seminary education. In order to return to seminary, Fr. Berschied had to give up all of his retirement money and use a good bit of his savings to pay for expenses not covered by the diocese. "When I returned to seminary," he recalls, "a lay friend in the parish reminded me of that verse in Scripture that says 'When you put your hand to the plow, don't look back' " (cf. Luke 9:62).

Without looking back, Fr. Berschied "plowed" through the difficulties of seminary life in the 1980s and was ordained in 1986. For the first few years of priesthood, his bishop assigned him to schools, first as a religion teacher and later as a principal. "Being a priest/religion teacher," he says, "is fairly natural and simply allows a priest to teach what he believes and lives. That particular role has the potential to allow the priest to give the Faith to the students in a unique and quite positive way. Although there was the occasional discipline problem, they were few and far between. Overall, I found the experience quite good, and I still enjoy making visitations to the classrooms in the elementary school in my parish."

Being a priest/school principal was a little more difficult, he admits. Although overall the experience was good in terms of being able to run a school as close as possible to the gospel, Fr. Berschied remembers the difficulties with dealing with all of the discipline problems and the parental complaints: "I remember being resisted by parents and students by requiring students to take Latin — which is proven to raise ACT and SAT scores, as well as improving personal speech, grammar, and language skills. I also remember being resisted by parents and students when I required all students to take a one-semester class in keyboarding/typing — and this was in 1988!

"I think a priest/school principal would work better if there were an assistant to handle the discipline problems. The priest could focus on the overall spiritual and academic tone of the school."

Priests and religious in Catholic schools are essential to continue the mission of the Church, Fr. Berschied adds. Even though there is a shortage of both at this time in some areas, in the long run, there would be a greater benefit to having some priests and religious in schools in order to develop future vocations.

In the meantime, Fr. Berschied will continue doing his share, with his hand to the plow, not looking back.

Postscript

Meeting the Challenge, Answering the Call

One of the big questions today about the priesthood in the Catholic Church is, how will the institution continue to survive? The sexual-abuse scandals that have blown up in the United States and elsewhere in recent years, and the accompanying culture of denial they've exposed, make this, from a strictly human perspective, a fair question.

In one way or another, each of the priests in the preceding chapters touched on many of the issues pertinent to the crisis that the priesthood faces today. One common thread that runs throughout each priest's comments is that the problems in the priesthood will not be solved by redefining or eliminating the priesthood — as some commentators have been urging for decades. *The priesthood itself is not the problem.* It is abuse within the ranks of the priesthood, burning like a brush fire, that is more often than not the true problem.

The solution must be rooted in fidelity to the Church's teachings, on faith and morals especially. In other words, one of the prerequisites to a strong, effective priesthood is *orthodoxy,* that is, a strong belief in and adherence to the Christian doctrines as taught by the Catholic Church. (You'd think this should go without saying, but at the beginning of the twenty-first century, it nonetheless remains to some ears a controversial assertion.)

Building on this basic prerequisite is *orthopraxis*, that is, putting into practice what one believes. Good works ought to flow from right belief, or, as Fr. Hinds called it, "sound theology," because faith without good works is a dead faith. These good works in the priesthood are realized in a number of ways, as the priests featured in this book have attested. Use of the human and theological virtues has always proven a good starting point. One particular virtue deserves special mention in a postscript of this sort in a book dealing with the Catholic priesthood. That virtue is fortitude.

Fr. Vaverek mentioned that the priesthood is not for the "faint of heart." Fr. McCloskey used a military metaphor to describe the kind of fortitude necessary for the aspiring priest. Priests, he said, are "the Navy Seals, the Army Rangers, the Green Berets of the Catholic Church." Fr. Perrone echoed this notion. He, too, relied on a military metaphor to describe how to respond to the incredible challenges faced by those who pursue a vocation to the priesthood in today's Church. In encouraging priestly vocations, he suggested, "we need to appeal to the young man's sense of idealism and dedication, much as the Marines do." One way of doing this is by informing the man of the heroic virtue that's required of a priest in any day and age, but especially at the outset of the twenty-first century. "Young men want a challenge," said Fr. Perrone. "It would be an understatement to say that the priesthood is a challenge."

The future of the priesthood is as much about attracting the "right men" — courageous and heroic men — as it is about weeding out those who do not belong. "Men are either attracted to the challenge of the priesthood," said Fr. Hinds, "or they are attracted to comfort. We've got to weed out the guys who are attracted to comfort, and we've got to nurture the men who are attracted to the challenge."

The basic formula for a strong priesthood, then, is fidelity and fortitude. A priest's fidelity and fortitude have the greatest of ramifications. The souls of many are placed in the care of the priest. Jesus Christ set up His Church as a hierarchical institution for a reason, using the metaphor of the shepherd and his sheep. Even a so-called "enlightened" laity needs moral and spiritual direction and proper moral guidance. If the shepherd is sick, the sheep suffer.

The layman must never forget, however, that the seeds of vocations to the priesthood are planted and grow in families and in parishes, primarily among laypersons. Fortitude, then, is just as important for laymen in the promotion of vocations as it is for priests. With fortitude, one ought to embrace the Cross, answer the call to more personal prayer, and be more strongly supportive of the guiding principles of the Church and the teachings of Christ.

At the same time, all Catholics would do well to bear in mind the four marks of a vocation, as elucidated by Fr. Gould: prayer, hard work, generosity, and sacrifice. To meet the challenge and answer the call, aspiring priests must see these four marks as viable within their own families and in their own parishes.

Michael S. Rose

Michael S. Rose is the author of three previous books, including the *New York Times* bestseller *Goodbye, Good Men* and *Ugly as Sin*. Over the past decade, he has emerged as one of the freshest new voices in the Catholic world. As a reporter and editorialist, he has illuminated a number of highly controversial issues in contemporary Catholicism. His many articles have appeared in venues such as *The Wall Street Journal*, *New York Newsday*, *The American Conservative*, and *Homiletic and Pastoral Review*. Rose writes regularly as an international news correspondent for *Catholic World Report* and serves as a contributing editor to *New Oxford Review*. A graduate of the University of Cincinnati and Brown University, Rose is married with four children and lives in Cincinnati.

Sophia Institute Press®

Sophia Institute® is a nonprofit institution that seeks to restore man's knowledge of eternal truth, including man's knowledge of his own nature, his relation to other persons, and his relation to God. Sophia Institute Press® serves this end in numerous ways: it publishes translations of foreign works to make them accessible to English-speaking readers; it brings out-of-print books back into print; and it publishes important new books that fulfill the ideals of Sophia Institute®. These books afford readers a rich source of the enduring wisdom of mankind. Sophia Institute Press® makes these high-quality books available to the public by using advanced technology and by soliciting donations to subsidize its publishing costs. Your generosity can help Sophia Institute Press® to provide the public with editions of works containing the enduring wisdom of the ages. Please send your tax-deductible contribution to the address below.

For your free catalog, call:
Toll-free: 1-800-888-9344

Sophia Institute Press® ♦ Box 5284 ♦ Manchester, NH 03108
www.sophiainstitute.com

Sophia Institute® is a tax-exempt institution as defined by the
Internal Revenue Code, Section 501(c)(3). Tax I.D. 22-2548708.